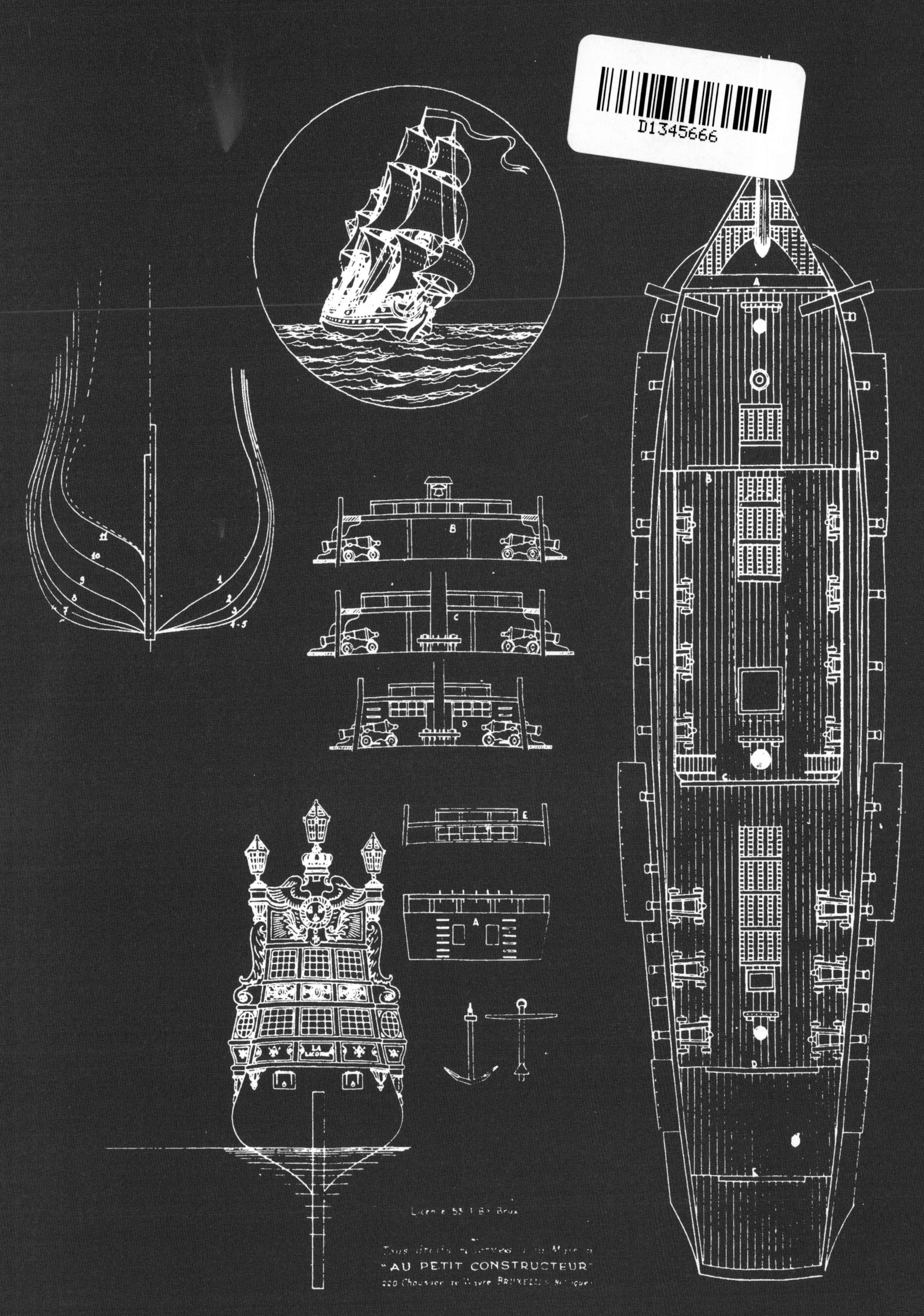
"AU PETIT CONSTRUCTEUR"

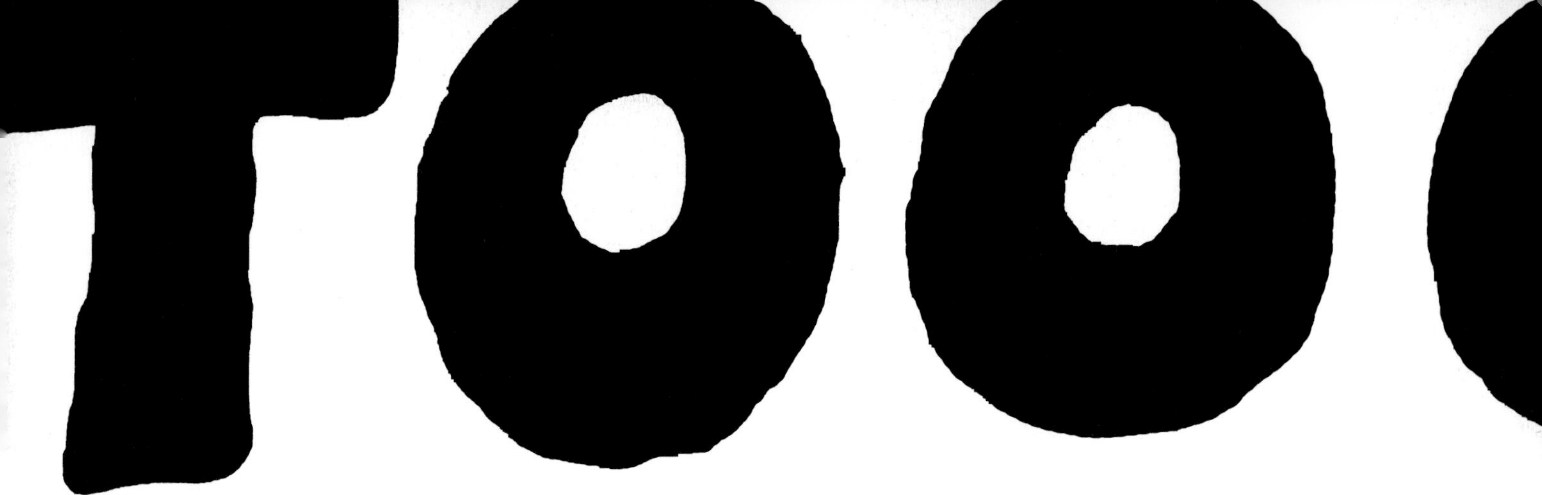

Like Tintin, I first took to the seas aboard a passenger liner bound for Africa. I travelled regularly with my parents in Union Castle ships, spending months of my early life absorbed by things maritime, if without the company of a small white dog and a black-bearded sea captain. I read my first Tintin book at the age of six. Hooked, I devoured every volume, and later spent years at sea with the Royal Navy experiencing adventures as exciting as any imagined by Hergé.

I am indebted to my friend Admiral Georges Prud'homme, then director of the Musée National de la Marine, who took me around his acclaimed Tintin exhibition in Paris a few years ago ('Mille Sabords!') and sparked the idea for our new show. It is delightful that Tintin is able to come to Greenwich exactly 75 years after his creation, and it is a privilege to work in partnership with the Fondation Hergé to interpret this fascinating and enjoyable character. I am very grateful to Nick Rodwell for his rapport with the Museum.

Since maritime museums were a rich source of information and inspiration for the adventures of Tintin, it is entirely appropriate for the National Maritime Museum to pay tribute to Hergé's legacy. Our exhibition draws on our diverse collections to demonstrate the author's painstaking research and characteristic attention to detail. The objects shown bring Tintin's world vividly to life, and we hope the stories will stimulate interest in maritime themes in visitors of all ages.

The exhibition benefits from the long-standing support of CP Ships in providing the gallery and from generous sponsorship by Ottakar's Bookstores and Egmont Books. I am very grateful to them all and in particular to James Heneage of Ottakar's for his personal commitment; he is a long-standing fan of Tintin and his shops take their name from a character in the stories.
The preparations within the Museum have been a team effort; I extend my gratitude to all, but with particular thanks to: David Spence for his leadership, Chris Walton for engaging our sponsors, and Robin Kiang, Sarah McCormick and Kristian Martin for handling many details and delivering the product.

Roy Clare
Director, National Maritime Museum
March 2004

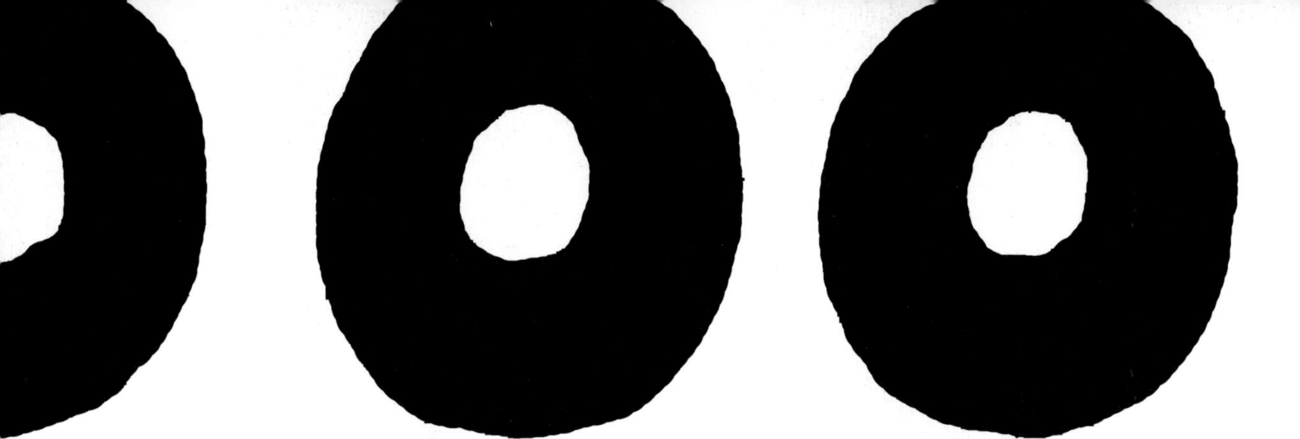

YVES HOREAU

THE ADVENTURES OF
TINTIN
AT SEA

Edited and translated by Michael Farr

Tintin at the National Maritime Museum

Less than ten years after their first adventure in the Soviet Union, Tintin and his little dog Snowy arrived in Dover on the cross-Channel ferry. *The Black Island*, begun in 1937, saw the young reporter travelling to Britain in search of a gang of forgers and a legendary beast. Although Tintin never visited London in his adventures – *The Black Island* was based largely in the Scottish Highlands – his creator enjoyed spending time in the capital for both business and pleasure. Hergé was a great Anglophile. He loved traditional English style and customs, and often bought his immaculately tailored suits and shirts on visits to London, which also allowed him to escape the pressures that fame had brought him in Brussels.

The National Maritime Museum, which holds a collection of over two million objects relating to the sea, ships, time and the stars

It is very likely that, during these sporadic visits, Hergé casually collected information on places of interest that was used in the Tintin stories, although much of the first edition of *The Black Island* was drawn from his imagination. However, when the adventure was redrawn in 1966, at the request of Tintin's English publishers, Hergé's trusted collaborator Bob De Moor undertook two weeks of intensive research in Britain, eventually retracing Tintin's steps to ensure that the new edition was accurate and up to date.

During his travels in Britain and the rest of Europe, Hergé enjoyed visiting museums, and his many files of correspondence show that they were a rich source of information and inspiration. In Paris they included the Musée National de la Marine, from which Hergé ordered ship plans and photographs to draw accurately a range of vessels in the Tintin adventures. There are also a few letters to and from British museums. It is not known whether any of Hergé's trips included a visit to the National Maritime Museum, and there is no record of whether he wrote to the Museum for information or advice. Being a French-speaker, however, he would naturally have gravitated towards the maritime museum in Paris for nautical information.

Yet, as we would expect, some of the cuttings in Hergé's vast research archive are of objects from the National Maritime Museum's collection, such as ship models which had been published in magazines and journals over the years. The Museum also became directly involved with Tintin during the 1950s, when it was approached by the English translators, Michael Turner and Leslie Lonsdale-Cooper. At the time they were translating *The Secret of the Unicorn* (1943), one of the richest of Tintin's maritime adventures, for which the Museum was happy to advise on details of Sir Francis Haddock's battle with pirates and the nautical vocabulary which now peppers this episode.

The diverse collections of the National Maritime Museum perfectly illustrate Hergé's sources of inspiration and the accuracy found in his work. *The Adventures of Tintin at Sea* exhibition brings alive Tintin's maritime exploits, enabling us to experience the reality behind the comic strips that we know and love. With a little imagination, the binnacle from the bridge of the *Ramona*, the sword and pistol belonging to Sir Francis Haddock, and the diving helmet used by Tintin to explore the wreck of the *Unicorn* can all be found in the Museum's collections.

Left,
Full hull model of a seventeenth-century Dutch two-decker warship

The Adventures at Sea Begin

By 1940 Tintin had already been to the Soviet Union, the Belgian Congo, America, Egypt, China and Britain, but his experiences at sea had so far been somewhat limited. He had travelled on various vessels – mainly passenger liners and ferries – predominately as a means of getting from Belgium to the setting for his current adventure. For Tintin's ninth adventure, however, Hergé planned that a large part of the story would take place at sea as Tintin was sent on the trail of villainous drug smugglers. It soon became clear to Hergé that, to enable him to exploit the potential of this thrilling watery environment, and for Tintin to thrive in a maritime world, he would need to create a companion for his hero who was comfortable and proficient at sea. This character came in the shape of Captain Archibald Haddock.

In *The Crab with the Golden Claws* (1941) Tintin meets Captain Haddock as he tries to escape from imprisonment on the cargo ship *Karaboudjan*. Plied with whisky by a mutinous crew, Haddock is initially presented as a sad and hopeless drunkard, the familiar and comical stereotype of the 'salty sea dog'. Hergé's wife suggested an appropriate name for this character. Over dinner she described a haddock as 'a sad English fish', which fitted perfectly with the qualities that Hergé was trying to portray in Haddock's first appearance.

During the following stories Haddock develops into a fascinating and lovable character. Tintin's friendship proves to be his salvation as he is weaned off the whisky (to some extent) and gradually drawn into his friend's turbulent life. We learn that the captain is a skilled sailor of noble maritime ancestry, and it soon becomes apparent that he is fundamentally a decent and loyal human being. His impulsive and explosive nature, however, is the antithesis of Tintin's character, and is the focus of much of the comedy in the tales. Nevertheless, Haddock becomes Tintin's loyal companion and confidant, and a pivotal character in inspiring the rich maritime adventures that followed.

In later years Hergé switched his attentions somewhat from Tintin to Haddock as the captain became the character that he most closely identified with. Haddock became an effective vehicle for Hergé to indulge his fantasies and escape some of the realities of life. He reflected many of Hergé's feelings and his desire to step on board a ship and explore the world. Indeed, some of the incidents that befell the captain were inspired by events in Hergé's own life and, through Haddock, Hergé was able to respond to real-life annoyances with a tirade of colourful abuse – 'billions of blistering barnacles', 'two-timing Tartar twisters' – something he could only dream of doing in reality.

Hey, Snowy, just look at that big star.
Which one?

Tintin and the Stars

With the publication of *The Shooting Star* in 1942, Tintin's world suddenly became Technicolor. The book was the very first of his adventures to be published in full colour. Hergé wasted no time in taking advantage of this new feature. The temptation may have been to colour every frame vividly and garishly, but Hergé was restrained yet bold in his approach. He used colour carefully, to accentuate the stories and give adjacent pages balance and harmony, without compromising the striking clarity of line in his drawings.

The Shooting Star opens with a night-time walk during which Tintin points out to Snowy an unusual star in the Great Bear constellation (*Ursa Major*). Upon further investigation at the local observatory, the star is revealed to be a giant meteorite on a collision course with the Earth. The sense of impending doom that opens Tintin's tenth adventure is both unexpected and disturbing. Yet Hergé's book captured perfectly the prevailing mood of despondency and menace being felt in occupied Belgium at this time.

These pages are characterized by a number of beautiful frames which depict Tintin against a star-filled night sky. The frames are even more outstanding in Hergé's original drawing, where they are extended to capture the enormity of the heavens.

Table celestial globe made by George Philip & Son of London, *circa* 1960

As well as demonstrating Hergé's great skill in composition and his restrained use of colour, these drawings also show how his desire for authenticity extended beyond the explicitly maritime world.

A search through Hergé's archive reveals a number of clippings of stars and constellations taken from scientific publications. They hint at the careful preparation and research that characterizes much of his work. Interestingly, Hergé used an Italian star chart to work out the exact arrangement of stars in the sky over Brussels at a particular time of the year: the chart has been marked by the points of Hergé's geometric compass, which he used to identify the correct portion of sky and stars to appear in these frames.

When *The Shooting Star* was transferred from comic strip to book, extra space allowed Hergé to add new illustrations, such as the large frame of a telescope dome on page 3. This was drawn from a photograph in Hergé's archive of the then largest telescope in the world, at the Mount Wilson Observatory in California. When depicting the observatory dome silhouetted against the night sky on page 2, Hergé also drew inspiration from his local observatory, the Royal Observatory of Belgium, at Uccle in Brussels. It is highly likely that such astronomy-related archives were again made use of a decade later, when Hergé sent Tintin into space in *Destination Moon* (1953) and its follow-up, *Explorers on the Moon* (1954).

That's it... Let's go in, and I'll work it out...

THE GREENWICH MERIDIAN

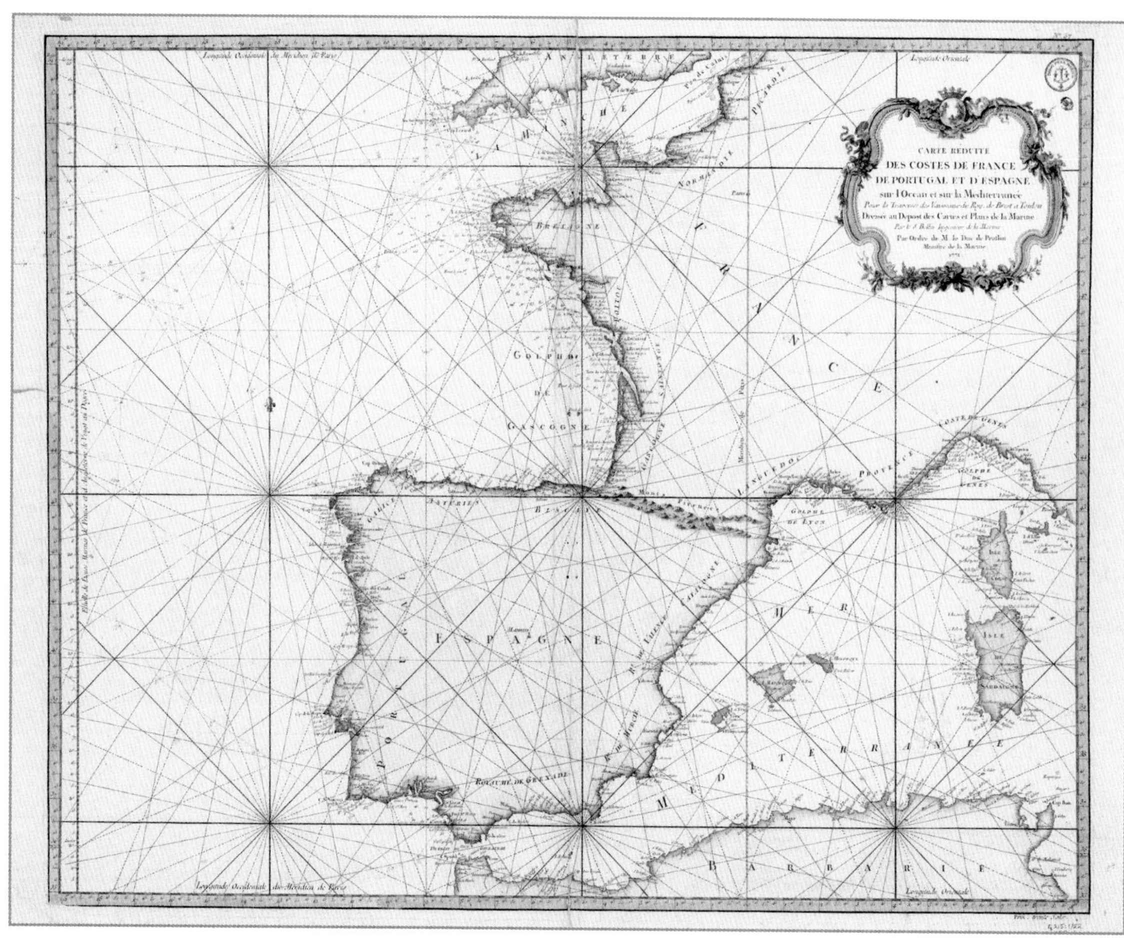

Chart of western Europe showing the meridian running through Paris as the prime meridian, by Jacques Nicolas Bellin, 1771

Hergé considered *The Secret of the Unicorn* and its sequel, *Red Rackham's Treasure*, to be among his finest work. Many of today's Tintin fans would certainly agree. The two books are the most nautical of the adventures, delving into naval history and presenting a complex voyage of discovery. Hergé's archive suggests that these were perhaps two of the most painstakingly researched stories. It is also clear that he enjoyed working on them, revelling in his deep fascination with the maritime world and showing how comfortable he felt in tackling some complicated issues that arise at sea.

One particular episode in *Red Rackham's Treasure* perfectly demonstrates the lengths to which Hergé went in his pursuit of accuracy and a credible story. During a voyage to locate pirate treasure, Captain Haddock and Tintin get lost and find that they are unable to locate the island where they believe the treasure is buried. According to the coordinates in clues left by the captain's ancestor Sir Francis Haddock, the island should be close by. It does not appear on their chart, however, and cannot be seen from the ship. Doubting their actual location, an experienced Captain Haddock checks their position using a sextant and discovers that they have indeed passed the correct point. Surprisingly, it is Tintin and not Haddock who solves the mystery. He suggests that Sir Francis Haddock's calculation was based on a seventeenth-century French chart marked with the Paris meridian rather than the Greenwich meridian.

Hergé had obviously researched and become interested in the problems associated with longitude. He was correct that the Greenwich meridian had not been officially selected as the Prime Meridian of the world – Longitude 0° – during Sir Francis Haddock's life: this took place at the International Meridian Conference in 1884. Before this date there was no international standardized fixed point on charts from which to measure distance and time. Depending on where a chart was produced, different lines of longitude were marked as the prime meridian, although the majority of sea charts available before 1884 did use the Greenwich meridian, owing to the great importance of London to international commerce.

The Paris meridian – today 2° 34' east – was just one of the lines sometimes marked as 0°, particularly on charts made in France. In fact it continued to be used on French charts up until 1911, as France initially refused to recognize Greenwich as the universal Prime Meridian. This caused difficulties for mariners, as there were many chart-makers in many countries producing charts for many voyages. As there was no consistency in the positioning of the prime meridian, the confusion experienced by Tintin and Captain Haddock would have been a real problem, as misunderstandings could potentially result in ships being lost and wrecked at sea.

Kristian Martin

Tintin had the good fortune to be born at the end of the 1920s, a time when there was still room for the adventurer and globe-trotter.

HERGÉ BOARDS THE MARITIME WORLD

Hergé himself, working in a newspaper office, had a particular regard for the foreign correspondent dispatched to remote corners of the world to report on little-known affairs. It was a role that he himself may have aspired to and that he was somehow able to achieve by creating a character, Tintin, who would meet the challenges on his behalf.

So at his creation, on 10 January 1929, Tintin, a young reporter accompanied by his faithful fox terrier, Snowy, left Brussels by train for Moscow, capital of a Soviet empire full of wild unknowns and uncertainties, rife with danger.

It was the age of the globe-trotter. Transport had improved, but not so much as to diminish the sense of adventure. While it was the age of the aeroplane, with every year recording pioneering achievements in aviation, for the long-distance traveller the principal means of transport remained the steamship. This was also the golden age of the ocean liner: the *Queen Mary*, the *Queen Elizabeth*, the *Normandie*. No sooner was Tintin back safely from Moscow than he boarded a steamer to the Congo, Belgium's vast African colony, and once he had finished with Africa he was soon aboard a transatlantic liner bound for New York. From then on ships and the sea were to form an integral part of *The Adventures of Tintin*.

Who were the intrepid travellers of the time? There were adventurers exploring the last uncharted areas of the globe; there were diplomats and businessmen plying back and forth on the steamship routes or the airlines linking major cities. There were audacious writers who sought distant and exotic destinations for their inspiration. There were the foreign correspondents sent to this or that destination by their editors to glean news. In Britain one could mention Malcolm Muggeridge writing from Russia, or Evelyn Waugh from Abyssinia; in Belgium one would, like Hergé, have in mind Albert Londres and Joseph Kessel, undoubtedly models for Tintin.

Then there were the men and women who aspired to beat world speed or height records, or to achieve one of the 'firsts' still to be attained.

A good ten years had passed since the Great War, and nations were competing – peacefully for the time being – to conquer the impossible. In short, the most diverse teams and individuals gave the world a hitherto unknown dynamism in these years.

From his first appearance in January 1929, Tintin is one of this band of enthusiastic pioneers. As for transport, he uses every means possible in the pursuit of his adventures. On land he takes express trains, goods trains, sports cars, racing cars, simple saloons, motorcycles, trucks, taxis, armoured cars, tanks, bicycles, rickshaws, sedan chairs, horses, camels, >

INTRODUCTION

mules and the back of an elephant. In the air, he flies airliners, flying boats, fighter planes, seaplanes, recreational aircraft, helicopters and, most memorably, a rocket to the moon.

As for the sea and water, Tintin is as naturally in his element travelling by ocean liner, battle-cruiser, cargo ship, oil tanker, converted trawler, miniature submarine, motor launch, speedboat, sambuk, fishing boat, lifeboat, canoe, raft or even floating coffin. He is a natural sailor – all the more so after he meets Captain Haddock in *The Crab with the Golden Claws* – and a good part of his adventures are at sea.

In the first adventure, *Tintin in the Land of the Soviets*, he takes possession of an armed motor launch. Next he travels by steamship to Africa and negotiates the river Congo by canoe; then it's on to America by transatlantic liner, with a diversion on a motor launch on Lake Michigan. He returns to Europe on one of the newest and most impressive of liners, the *Normandie*.

The Middle and Far East beckon, and Tintin boards another liner – this time for Egypt. Unexpectedly cast adrift in a coffin on the Red Sea, he is picked up by a sambuk, a local coaster. Via India, he makes his way to China for *The Blue Lotus* – by steamship there and back, but including a short trip on a junk. For the next adventure, Tintin sets out from Le Havre for the fictional South American republic of San Theodoros, once again by transatlantic liner. There he travels downriver by canoe, before returning home by steamship. He catches up with another transatlantic liner in his attempt to recover the fetish in *The Broken Ear*.

After such long sea voyages, the next adventure, *The Black Island*, is more modest, involving a Channel crossing aboard the Ostend-Dover ferry and the purchase of a fishing boat off the west coast of Scotland. The Balkan setting of *King Ottokar's Sceptre* does not allow for much navigation, apart from the use of a rowing boat and a return by flying boat, then in vogue as a luxurious means of passenger transport.

The looming war, presaged in *King Ottokar's Sceptre*, then became a reality, catching up with Hergé and Tintin in May 1940 with the Nazi invasion of Belgium. It was the second time in Hergé's lifetime that he had to endure the experience of having his home city occupied by Germans. But the change of circumstances led to one of the most maritime of the Tintin adventures, *The Crab with the Golden Claws*, where, perhaps only to Snowy's chagrin, Tintin meets the alcohol-sodden Captain Haddock, soon to become his closest friend and companion and, thanks to Tintin, most of the time a reformed character. The captain's presence in all the subsequent adventures ensured a nautical element even when much later, as in *The Castafiore Emerald*, there is an adventure with no travel involved.

The sea predominates in the adventures immediately following *The Crab with the Golden Claws*: *The Shooting Star*, *The Secret of the Unicorn* and *Red Rackham's Treasure*. For more than four years Tintin, Snowy and Haddock are to be found in the waters off the north coast of Africa and in the Arctic region, the Atlantic and the Caribbean. In fact for the whole period of the German occupation Tintin can be said to have been at sea – it allowed Hergé a form of escapism from the grim reality of his own world under the Nazi jackboot.

The question is why Hergé, essentially a landlubber, should have shown such affection for the sea and for things nautical. The answer probably lies in the enthusiasm of some of his friends, which clearly rubbed off. Then, as this book demonstrates, Hergé, true to his nature, became extremely conscientious in his preparation and study of maritime detail for use in the books. The result is an unusual degree of authenticity, which enhances the appeal of the adventures.

A number of factors have a bearing on Hergé's cycle of maritime adventures. As early as 1935 he took out a subscription to a nautical magazine whose illustrations he appreciated and could add to his swelling archive of material for possible future use. Two years later, through his work on calendars for the Federation of Catholic Scouts of Belgium, he met Gérard Liger-Belair, a naval historian and owner of a model-making business. In 1939 he moved from the Woluwe-Saint-Lambert quarter of Brussels (where, incidentally, he lived near a Sirius Close and a Close of the Unicorn) to the leafy district of Boitsfort on the outskirts of the city, where, a few hundred yards from his new home, there was a lake used by members of the Model Yacht Club of Brussels to sail their reduced-scale vessels. On Sunday mornings he would exchange pleasantries and information with some of the model-makers and some of the spectators. Among the latter was a particularly well-informed collector who soon invited him home and showed him his own maritime gallery, not far from the Old Market. On display was a remarkable collection of objects, of paintings and of reduced-scale models. The collector offered to furnish the creator of Tintin with any additional information should an adventure require it. The man was not called Ivan Sakharine - the collector in *The Secret of the Unicorn* - but he was just like him, and he and Hergé quickly became friends.

There was also a Brussels antique dealer called Loiseau who provided material, and another who, together with his sons, was preparing to open a private maritime museum in Brussels.

Hergé met and befriended all these enthusiasts, and some of them were to help weave the story of the life and destiny of Sir Francis Haddock, captain of the *Unicorn* and illustrious ancestor of Captain Haddock. It was one way for an author who had started with scarcely any nautical knowledge to go to sea for the enduring pleasure of his readers.

PHILIPPE GODDIN
and MICHAEL FARR

THE KARABOUDJAN

Hergé made up the name of this ship. On 20 September 1972 he wrote to his friend the author Gabriel Matzneff,

'One day when we meet again, you are sure to tell me that the name actually exists, though I thought I had invented it.'

As was his method, he brought together two names from one geographical region – KARA BOUgaz, a gulf on the east of the Caspian Sea, and AzerbaiDJAN – to produce, as Tintin notes, an Armenian-sounding name.

Later in the *The Crab with the Golden Claws* the name of the vessel is fraudulently changed to the *Djebel Amilah*, another invention. In this case Hergé seems to have been inspired by 'Djebel', the Maghrib transcription of the Arab word for a mountain, and the Algerian town of Djamila.

Rather less complicatedly, the actual ship is drawn from photographs in Hergé's possession of the Glasgow-registered cargo vessel *Glengarry*.

Photograph of the Glasgow-registered *Glengarry*

ESCAPE BY LIFEBOAT

Tintin and Haddock slip away from the *Karaboudjan* by lifeboat – a scene based on photographs in Hergé's collection showing survivors from the French liner *Georges-Philippar*, which sank in 1932 and included among her victims the well-known foreign correspondent Albert Londres, one of the inspirations behind Tintin.

THE AURORA

Hergé built up his collection of newspaper clippings and photographs of boats to enable him to depict vessels with increasing accuracy.

The source material he used for his two polar ships in *The Shooting Star* – the *Aurora*, which carries the name of a sealer which sailed on a number of Antarctic expeditions, and the *Peary* – is not certain. However, when Tintin climbs the ratlines to dislodge the mad 'prophet' Philippulus from the crow's-nest, Hergé has clearly been inspired by a couple of photographs: one showing a lookout in the rigging, another a ship's crow's-nest.

Similarly, the pitching of a vessel such as the *Aurora* is shown in a drawing he filed among his papers.

The fuelling of the *Aurora* via the *Sirius* reproduces a photograph showing the *Prince Baudouin* taking on fuel. There is also a photograph behind Hergé's portrait of the ship's engineer and the battery of dials in his engine room.

Nevertheless, Hergé was not satisfied with the *Aurora*. He told his interviewer Numa Sadoul, 'I regret that I did not think of using a model for drawing the *Aurora*. The boat I devised was not a great success. It would not have stayed afloat.'

Moreover, any sailor would note that, on the quayside, the gangplank is not properly secured.

Furthermore, on the forecastle of the *Aurora*, a cable is wound around an unrecognizable apparatus.

Finally, Hergé has omitted the derrick for the seaplane.

Sketches of a ship pitching to be found among Hergé's papers

An unknown apparatus
on the forecastle of the *Aurora*

THE UNICORN

A vessel of historic interest

A pencil sketch by Hergé

Tintin's polar expedition in* The Shooting Star *underlined to Hergé the difficulty of depicting realistically the different angles of a ship at sea.

Once he decided that a major episode in the new adventure, *The Secret of the Unicorn*, was to take place aboard a warship belonging to Louis XIV's navy – or, in the case of the English edition, a vessel belonging to the fleet of Charles II – there could be no question of improvisation. He gradually accumulated the necessary documentation on the historical context, as well as on the shipbuilding of the period.

With the benefit of the research undertaken on the *Unicorn* by Jean-Claude Lemineur, a naval historian specializing in the sixteenth and seventeenth centuries who is also a talented model-maker and Tintin enthusiast, we will try to uncover the probable sources that Hergé turned to and find out what he drew from them.

The historical context

The events recounted in *The Secret of the Unicorn* can be dated to 1698. The War of the League of Augsburg, which pitted the France of Louis XIV against a coalition of powerful European maritime nations, had just been concluded to France's disadvantage by the Treaty of Ryswick. While disadvantageous to France, the treaty required Spain to cede to it half of the island of Hispaniola – better known as Haiti or St Domingo – part of the Antilles archipelago. The administration and exploitation of this new overseas possession required a constant commercial and political link. A military presence to ensure the safe passage of trade was also needed, because of the proximity to Turtle Island, a well-known pirate haunt in the seventeenth century situated only about 38 nautical miles north of St Domingo. This task fell to the French navy, which dispatched a small force to carry out policing operations.

At its head were less formidable vessels of the third or fourth rank – though, compared with the largest commercial ships, they were impressive enough. A ship of the third rank would have 50-60 cannon and 250 men in peacetime, augmented to 350 men during war.

Unlike in Hergé's narrative, such a vessel should therefore have been more than capable of holding her own in a confrontation, and this type of ship guaranteed communications between Versailles and Port-au-Prince. The *Unicorn*, sailing in Caribbean waters bound for Europe, is returning from such a mission.

Hergé has not left many clues about the genesis of this nautical adventure set during the reign of Louis XIV. There are some suggestions and a few pencil sketches based on reduced-scale models belonging to a collector friend, or on unknown documents.

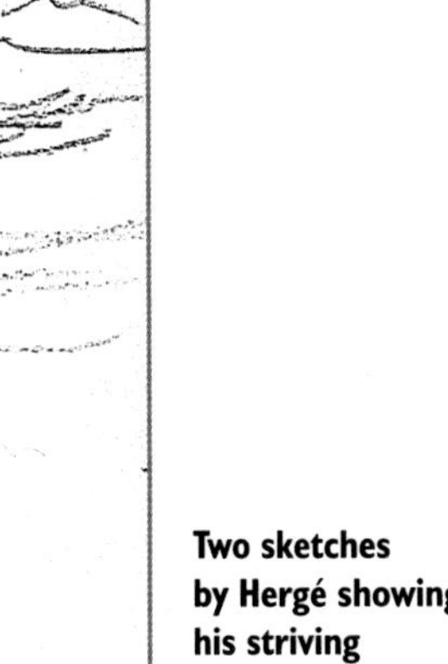

Two sketches by Hergé showing his striving for accuracy and authenticity

A preparatory sketch by Hergé

The poop of the *Unicorn*; Liger-Belair's plan

Berain's designs showing the stern of the *Brillant*

The adventure first unfolded in daily strips in the newspaper *Le Soir* between 11 June 1942 and 4 January 1943, and showed a three-masted vessel with a single row of gun hatches, about twenty cannon, and a stern with only one row of windows.

In the book that followed, such a vessel is still to be seen in the part of the narrative before the naval engagement. She was corrected, but even today she does not resemble the *Unicorn* portrayed on the book's cover or title page. However, for the naval battle Hergé did modify the broad lines of the ship: there are two batteries instead of one, but no more than 25 cannon altogether, and the poop is improved and more richly decorated, with two rows of four windows (compared with three today).

Gérard Liger-Belair recalls that, in a panic, Hergé ordered from him a blueprint and a model of a ship of the line at the time of Louis XIV, which would allow him to sketch the vessel in detail and at various angles. Furthermore, Hergé took care to show him his drawings, so that they could be corrected before publication. This blueprint was a plan published for Belgian model-makers, and had been on sale in Brussels for 30 years. Later, while not denying the assistance of Liger-Belair, Hergé maintained that he had his own documentation and that the model was made only after the event. Jean-Claude Lemineur shares this view. He considers that, while it is probable that Liger-Belair checked Hergé's drawings, clearly the bulk of the material used for the creation of the *Unicorn* came from the second volume of Admiral Paris's *Souvenirs de marine* (*Naval Memoirs*). This contained all the ingredients needed for re-creating a vessel belonging to Louis XIV's navy, even though it did not include an example of a vessel of the third rank.

The historic basis of his narrative obliged Hergé to depict the *Unicorn* as higher than a vessel of the third rank. Without an example of this type of ship – either in Admiral Paris's volume or in museum collections – Hergé opted for his own composite creation, based on the plans and decoration of a second-rank vessel, the *Brillant*. The transformation of this ship conceived for 60 cannon led him to reduce the artillery by suppressing five gun hatches on each side, thus cutting the cannon to 50. The decoration remained to be adapted, and, undoubtedly enchanted by that devised by Jean Berain in 1689 for the *Brillant*, Hergé copied much of it.

Nevertheless, thinking that a ship such as the *Unicorn* would probably have a narrower stern, he scaled down the design and eliminated two windows at each of the two levels and two gun hatches in the lower battery. For the decoration of the *Unicorn*'s poop, the general design of the *Brillant*'s panels, with fleurs-de-lis, shells, tracery and medallions, has been retained in simplified form. The sides are decorated with a ciborium also borrowed from the *Brillant*. The two caryatids – female busts with legs in the form of acanthus leaves – have been transformed into two large, complete acanthus leaves to support the cornice upon which the ship's side lanterns are placed, recalling the design of the original decoration. The size and decoration of the area for the latrines as created by Jean Berain is adopted without change by Hergé, and is also to be found on Liger-Belair's plan.

For the complex rigging, as well as the choice of colours, Hergé turned to another ship, the *Louis XV*, the details of which feature in Admiral Paris's magnificent work.

'In France,' he told Numa Sadoul, 'there had never been a ship called the *Unicorn*.'

This is only half true. It is a fact that in the seventeenth century no French vessel was given this name, but it was otherwise very common in the navy's history. The first French *Unicorn* appeared in 1549 in Dieppe, and subsequently there were fourteen warships bearing this name, often prize vessels incorporated into the fleet.

Apart from the *Unicorn*'s eminent position in the adventures of Tintin, this superb vessel marks an important stage in Hergé's creativity regarding maritime matters. For the first time his naval imagination is firmly rooted in reality: documents, plans, models. In future there would be no fanciful embarkations which could give rise to criticism from eagle-eyed nautical observers.

The *Unicorn* is to Hergé's ships what *The Blue Lotus* is to his other work: the first example of painstaking accuracy.

An original artillery piece

As for the artillery, Hergé shows a cannon with a seventeenth-century mounting of the type used by the French. However, the system depicted, using a heavy rope that checks the recoil of the gun by encircling the knob of the cannon's breech, is in the English manner. The French preferred to rope both gun-carriage cheeks to iron rings attached to either side of the gun hatch. Hergé is mistaken in attaching the rope only to the starboard side and then to a pulley hanging on the wall of the ship.

Hergé's illustration has additionally a container of cannon balls ranged along the side and a rammer at the feet of the gunner in charge, who is equipped with a smouldering-fuse lighter. There is also a bucket of water that would be used to cool the cannon. However, the team of three would be insufficient to man the gun for action. According to the norms of the period, this would require as many as ten men.

The uniform shown tallies with the relevant illustration in the Larousse encyclopaedia, except that there the bonnets are red and the trousers have blue stripes. However, this illustration appears only in the 1948 edition of Larousse – several years after the appearance of the strip cartoon – showing that Hergé derived his information from other sources. His rich detail demonstrates the extent of his research. Unfortunately, it is impossible to pin down the precise sources he used.

Why the name '*Unicorn*'?

Hergé preferred not to copy the figurehead of the *Brillant*, which was decorated with a figure of Fame as a siren, her legs becoming an undulating fish tail, and adorned with acanthus leaves. Instead he chose to use a unicorn, which he found had been the figurehead of an English frigate built in Plymouth in 1748, captured by the French in 1780, but recaptured the following year by the Royal Navy in the Caribbean, where she was taking part in Franco-Spanish naval operations between St Domingo, Jamaica, Cuba and the southern coast of the United States of America.

Hergé discovered the material on the frigate and her figurehead in Fredrik Henrik af Chapman's *Architectura Navalis Mercatoria*. During this period, the figureheads of ships often reflected their names. Moreover, Hergé was careful not to adopt a name that was already that of an authentic vessel in the navy of Louis XIV.

THE SIRIUS

The name chosen by Hergé for the ship in* Red Rackham's Treasure *is that of a celebrated British steamer which in 1838 became the first ship to cross the Atlantic entirely under steam, taking 18 days and 10 hours at an average speed of 6.7 knots.

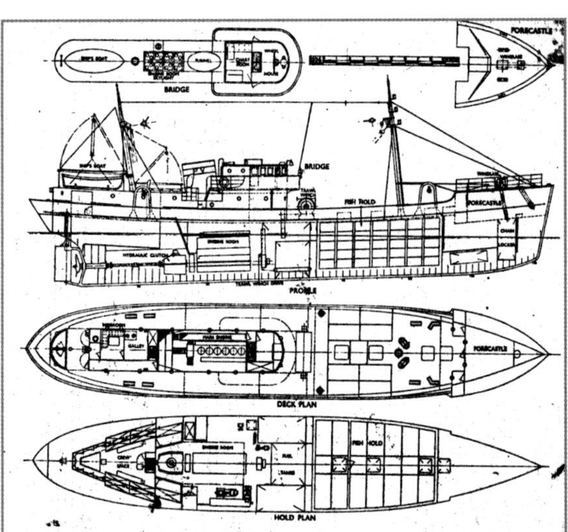

Plan of the *John – O.88* (O denotes Ostend)

We already caught a fleeting glimpse of the *Sirius* in *The Shooting Star*, though differences between the two depictions are apparent. Hergé's *Sirius* is again based on an actual vessel. Subscribing to a specialist magazine, Hergé had in 1936 spotted a photograph of an elegant trawler which had recently been put into service at Ostend, the *John – O.88*.

Later, while he was working on *Red Rackham's Treasure*, Hergé returned to the photograph of the *John – O.88* and reproduced a mirror image of it. But, as with the *Unicorn*, he decided to draw the details from a model. So he went to the shipyards of the builders, Jos Boel & Son, and came away with the plans of the trawler.

In addition to the plans, Hergé obtained from a collector a small-scale model cut away at the waterline. This enabled him to draw the *Sirius* from every angle, occasionally making modifications to the original.

For the detail, Hergé was able to draw on an increasingly abundant amount of material. Thus the windlass, pictured on the right, is copied from a photograph taken on board a steam trawler and found among his papers.

A model of the *Sirius* made in 1952 by A. Van Noeyen, to be found at the Hergé Foundation. It should not be confused with the first model acquired by Hergé when he was working on *Red Rackham's Treasure*

A photograph of the *John – O.88*, taken from a maritime magazine by Hergé

The *Ramona*

THE PACHACAMAC AND THE RAMONA

Once again, when drawing the* Pachacamac, *which is seen briefly in* Prisoners of the Sun, *Hergé went back to the Jos Boel & Son shipyard.

The *Pachacamac*

The shipbuilder provided him with photographs and a detailed plan of the SS *Egypt*, which had been begun as part of the German wartime 'Hansa' programme – a scheme similar to the American 'Liberty' programme that led to the building of the well-known 'Liberty ships' – and was completed in 1946.

This ship was already planned and under construction when the Boel shipyard was liberated by the Allies. She was delivered to a Belgian shipowner, Deppe Merchant Shipping, and when traffic resumed from the port of Antwerp she was used to transport oranges from Palestine.

The SS *Egypt* was then used as the model for the Panamanian cargo ship the *Ramona*, which is used scandalously as a slave transport in *The Red Sea Sharks*.

For the drawings of the interior of the *Pachacamac*, Hergé had gone on board a cargo vessel moored at Antwerp. This time for the *Ramona* he decided to go on a trip with Bob De Moor, his chief assistant, to enable them to make on-the-spot drawings. Accordingly, he contacted the maritime magazine where twenty years previously he had found the photograph of the trawler *John – O.88*, and it put him in touch with a shipping line whose vessels sailed regularly between Antwerp and Scandinavia.

So on 17 August 1956 Hergé and Bob De Moor embarked on the *Reine Astrid* for the four-day sailing between Antwerp and Göteborg. During the trip they took a large number of photographs and made numerous sketches that could be used for the *Ramona*.

ON BOARD WITH HERGÉ AND BOB DE MOOR

Drawings by Hergé based on photographs and sketches of the *Reine Astrid*

NAVAL ENCOUNTER ON THE RED SEA

The* Red Sea Sharks *represents the zenith of maritime adventure in Hergé's works. Tintin and Captain Haddock come across a cargo vessel, the* Ramona, *two warships, a submarine and the American cruiser USS* Los Angeles, *as well as a selection of other boats, all of which were carefully researched by Hergé.

The Scheherazade

The yacht belonging to Rastapopolous, alias the Marquis di Gorgonzola, is derived from a photograph of a boat that Hergé filed among his papers.

The Scheherazade's Launch

The motor launch belonging to the billionaire yacht-owner, which encloses a miniature submarine, is similar to the model employed in *The Calculus Affair* – for the good reason that they were both derived from the same ample archive of information that Hergé had accumulated on such craft.

Rastapopoulos's Pocket Submarine

The fantastic one-man submarine used by Rastapopoulos for his getaway is improbable, though Hergé did have a German newspaper clipping of a similar invention (see page 31).

The submarine

The pirate submarine codenamed *Shark*, commanded by Kurt – who had clearly served in the *Kriegsmarine* – is a type-VIIC U-boat dating from 1939. This model accounted for three-fifths of the Third Reich's flotilla.

Hergé was short of information on the appearance of periscope sightings. He combed libraries and asked his assistants, but came up with nothing until he found an English book entitled *A Submariner in the Royal Navy*.

He had plenty of information on torpedoes, but this did not prevent him from making a small technical error when he has the submarine manoeuvring underwater with her stem torpedo tubes open.

What interested Hergé in this photograph that he set aside was not the ship, which was not of the Baltimore class to which the USS *Los Angeles* belonged, but the sailors' uniforms, which he copied

The American Battlecruiser Los Angeles

Hergé copied the USS *Los Angeles* from a photograph that is no longer traceable in his archives. The heavy cruiser, belonging to the Baltimore class, was built in Philadelphia and launched on 20 August 1944.

One should note that in 1956, when Hergé was working on this adventure, much Second World War military material, whether American or German, was becoming out of date. However, information on and designs for the latest equipment – both ships and aircraft – would not have been available, remaining classified as military secrets.

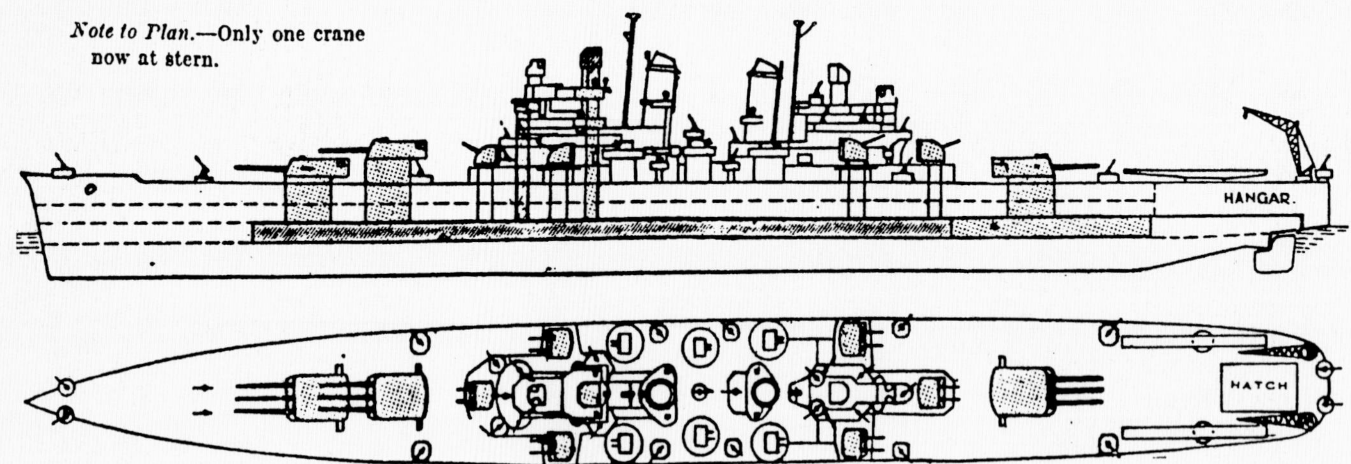

The sambuk Arab coasters

The Red Sea Sharks includes a couple of these fine two-masted coasters which ply Arabian waters so colourfully. Their raised sterns make them reminiscent of early fishing caravels.

'It's a dhow ... No, sorry, it's a sambuk,' says the captain, even though he could not claim to be an expert on the various vessels that sail the Red Sea. He should have said, 'It's a dhow, or to be precise a sambuk', as 'dhow' – an Indian word – is the term used for all the boats characterized by their trapezoidal sails which sail alongside the Arabian peninsula. Among the dhows there are several varieties of sailing boat, such as the ghanja with three masts, the dhum with two masts and no superstructure, and the baggala and sambuk (an Arabic name), with two masts and a raised stern, sometimes resembling European merchant vessels of the seventeenth century.

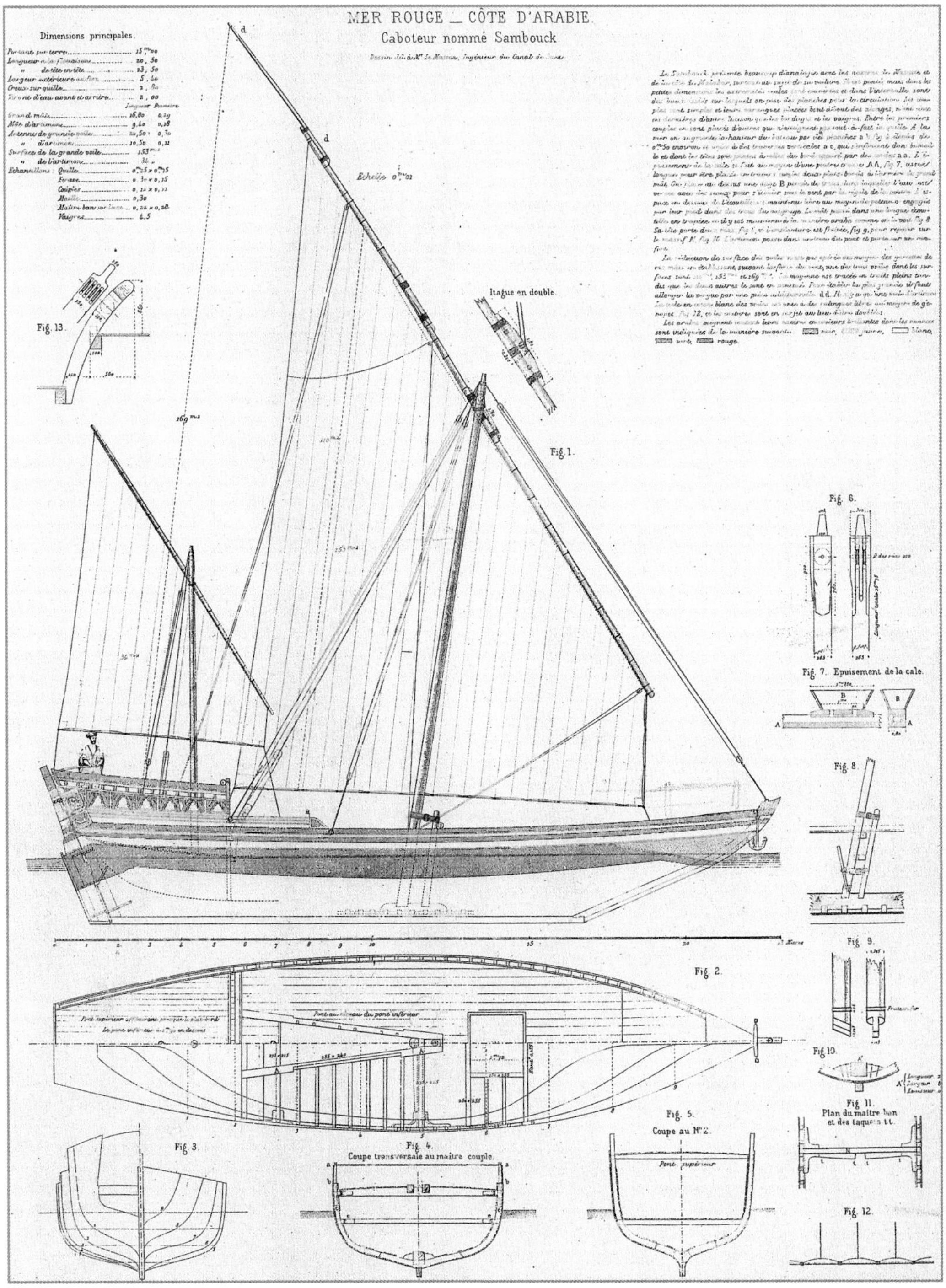

MER ROUGE _ CÔTE D'ARABIE
Caboteur nommé Sambouck

HERGÉ'S UNDERWATER WORLD

The archives built up by Hergé include a number of folders on underwater flora and fauna, as well as photographs and articles on the wreck of the *Vasa*, the Swedish seventeenth-century ship that was found preserved in silt and later refloated. While this archaeological discovery clearly excited Hergé, he interpreted his material with considerable freedom.

Fish depicted in *Red Rackham's Treasure* were copied from attractive watercolours of the pink and red cabrilla, or sea bass, which are to be found in the waters of the Canary Islands.

The jellyfish were drawn from photographs, while the diving suits – and the difficulty of moving in one – are fastidiously reproduced from images that Hergé collected.

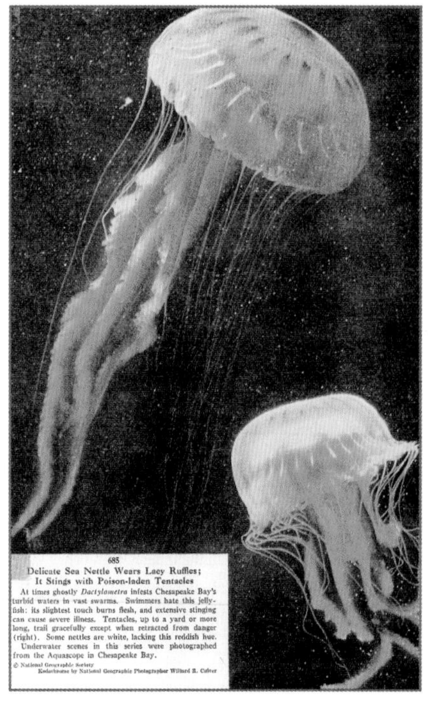

685

Delicate Sea Nettle Wears Lacy Ruffles;
It Stings with Poison-laden Tentacles

At times ghostly *Dactylometra* infests Chesapeake Bay's turbid waters in vast swarms. Swimmers hate this jellyfish: its slightest touch burns flesh, and extensive stinging can cause severe illness. Tentacles, up to a yard or more long, trail gracefully except when retracted from danger (right). Some nettles are white, lacking this reddish hue.

Underwater scenes in this series were photographed from the Aquascope in Chesapeake Bay.

© National Geographic Society

Kodachrome by National Geographic Photographer Willard R. Culver

The Pocket Submarine

Though inspired to some extent by Professor Auguste Piccard's bathyscaphe, as Hergé acknowledged in his interviews with Numa Sadoul, the one-man submarine developed by Professor Calculus in *Red Rackham's Treasure* was essentially original. However, Hergé did possess a German newspaper article about a similar craft created by an American inventor at around the time of *Red Rackham's Treasure*. If this was a little late for Professor Calculus, it could have influenced the mini-submarine used by Rastapopoulos for his unexpected escape in *The Red Sea Sharks*.

Mit 12 „Sachen" durchs Wasser. Kaum ist der Taucher festgeschnallt und die Klappe geschlossen (rechts), hebt sich „Mini Sub" vom Boden und gleitet, von einem Elektromotor angetrieben, mit 12 Stundenkilometern durchs Wasser. Wer gerne Rad fährt, kann das Boot auch mit Pedalantrieb bekommen. Sportler und Forscher brauchen keine Angst vor Haifischen mehr zu haben…

THE SHIPS MENTIONED AND DEPICTED

In The Adventures of Tintin there are two ships which bear the names of famous people: Washington, who of course also gave his name to a town, a city and a state, and Peary, after whom the Peary Land region of Greenland is named.

Generally Hergé preferred to avoid using the names of actual people, to prevent political, religious or cultural controversy and to enhance Tintin's internationalism. For the most part he therefore chose names for his ships that were based on geography or mythology.

AURORA

(The Shooting Star)

A polar ship bearing the name of an actual sealer that served on Arctic expeditions. Her mission in the Tintin adventure is to recover the meteorite that has plunged into Arctic waters.

DJEBEL AMILAH

(The Crab with the Golden Claws)

The new name which the *Karaboudjan* (see below) is illicitly given. While it does not refer to any known mountain, it seems to have been inspired by the Algerian town of Djamila.

EPOMEO (in the original French) / **ISIS** (in the English translation)

(Cigars of the Pharaoh)

The liner which takes Tintin and Snowy to Egypt. 'Epomeo' is also the name of a mountain on the island of Ischia, facing Naples. The English edition prefers *Isis*, the name of an Egyptian goddess, sister and wife of Osiris and mother of Horus.

HARIKA MARU

(The Blue Lotus)

The ship operated by the Japanese villain Mitsuhirato to supply opium to Marseilles. Moored in Shanghai opposite hangar no. 9, to which Tintin hastens only to fall into a trap.

KARABOUDJAN

(The Crab with the Golden Claws)

A cargo ship transporting opium – unknown to her captain (Haddock), who in an alcoholic stupor has allowed the first mate, Allan Thompson, to take control. The ship's name would seem to be derived from two places in the same part of the world: Kara Bougaz and Azerbaidjan. The ship is later disguised as the *Djebel Amilah* (see above).

KENTUCKY STAR

(The Shooting Star)

Given a name with an obvious American derivation, this boat attempts but fails to ram and sink the *Aurora*.

LOS ANGELES

(The Red Sea Sharks)

A United States Navy battle-cruiser built in Philadelphia and launched in 1944. Reproduced very faithfully by Hergé. Like a guardian angel, she saves Tintin, Haddock and their cargo of liberated slaves from the mephistophelean Rastapopolous, alias the Marquis di Gorgonzola.

PACHACAMAC

(Prisoners of the Sun)

A Peruvian cargo ship sailing between the ports of Callao and La Rochelle. She bears the name of the sun, venerated by the Incas, as well as of a sacred Andean town. Hergé's depiction is based on the SS *Egypt*, 1,862 tons, completed in 1946 by the Belgian shipbuilder Jos Boel & Son as part of the wartime 'Hansa' programme undertaken by the Germans.

PEARY

(The Shooting Star)

An American polar vessel in the first edition, racing the *Aurora* to recover the meteorite from Arctic waters. In subsequent editions she changes nationality to the fictional São Rico. The name is that of the American explorer of Greenland who in 1909 became the first man to reach the North Pole.

RAMONA

(The Red Sea Sharks)

A Panamanian-registered cargo vessel commanded by Captain Haddock's former first mate, Allan Thompson, engaged in the transport as slaves to Arabia of gullible Africans believing themselves to be on a pilgrimage to Mecca. As with the *Pachacamac* (see above), the SS *Egypt* provided the model.

RANCHI

(The Blue Lotus)

The liner on which Tintin departs from Shanghai. Ranchi is a town in the north of India.

SCHEHERAZADE

(The Red Sea Sharks)

A luxury yacht belonging to Rastapopolous, alias the Marquis di Gorgonzola. Michael Farr has found that it is closely modelled on the celebrated *Christina*, owned by Aristotle Onassis, which was very much in the news at the time when Hergé was working on this adventure and about which he gathered material. Scheherazade is, of course, the legendary storyteller in *The Arabian Nights' Entertainments*.

SERENO

(Cigars of the Pharaoh)

A still from a film exists as the prototype for this small yacht captained by Haddock's former deputy Allan Thompson, who takes on board Tintin, Snowy and Professor Sarcophagus boxed in coffins.

SIRIUS

(The Shooting Star, Red Rackham's Treasure)

A trawler commanded by Haddock's old friend Captain Chester in *The Shooting Star*. Chester lends her to Haddock for his treasure-hunting expedition in *Red Rackham's Treasure*. She bears the name of a famous nineteenth-century English steamer, and was drawn by Hergé from a model and plans of an Ostend trawler, the *John – O.88*, built in 1936 by the Belgian shipyard of Jos Boel & Son.

Speedol Star
(Land of Black Gold)
A tanker sailing between Europe and the Middle East. Tintin is employed as the ship's radio operator, and the Thom(p)sons are sailors on board. Hergé drew the ship from material he had in his archives, but was not fully satisfied. He therefore sent his trusted assistant Bob De Moor to the port of Antwerp to sketch and photograph a tanker dating from 1939. The ship was subsequently redrawn in 1971.

Unicorn
(The Secret of the Unicorn)
A man-of-war of the third rank commanded by the chevalier François de Hadoque serving in the navy of France's Louis XIV in the original French version, or by Sir Francis Haddock, admiral in the navy of His Britannic Majesty Charles II, in the English edition.

Ville de Lyon
(The Broken Ear)
A transatlantic liner sailing between the French port of Le Havre and South America, in this case the fictional San Theodoros. The ship is destroyed by fire while Tintin is in Nuevo Rico.

Washington
(The Broken Ear)
A transatlantic liner sailing between Europe and the Americas.

Ships mentioned but not shown

Benares
(The Crab with the Golden Claws)
A steamer which tries unsuccessfully to help the *Karaboudjan*.

Black Cat
(The Seven Crystal Balls)
A ship which is loaded at La Rochelle in the original French, or at the fictional Bridgeport in the English edition.

Black Star
(The Blue Lotus)
A ship operated by Mitsuhirato, carrying opium, bound for Rotterdam.

Cithara
(The Shooting Star)
A non-existent ship in distress whose SOS signal is put out by the *Peary* to delay and divert the *Aurora* from her quest to recover the meteorite.

The following vessels respond to Tintin's message asking for information on ships whose names begin with 'Cit ...' and whether they are in distress: **Cithern, Cità di Verona, Citoyenne Louise, City of Bath, City of Exeter, City of Lincoln, City of Oxford.**

Everest
(The Blue Lotus)
A ship operated by Mitsuhirato, carrying opium, bound for Hamburg.

Jupiter
(The Crab with the Golden Claws)
A merchant vessel which, according to a radio report, runs aground in severe gales.

Marigold
(The Blue Lotus)
A ship operated by Mitsuhirato, carrying opium, bound for Marseilles.

Saturn
(The Blue Lotus)
A ship operated by Mitsuhirato, carrying opium, bound for Liverpool.

Tanganyika
(The Crab with the Golden Claws)
A steamship which sinks near Vigo in severe gales, according to a radio report. Her crew are rescued.

Titanic
(Red Rackham's Treasure, Land of Black Gold)
'You see that, eh? I suppose it's the figurehead of the TITANIC!' an exasperated Captain Haddock declares to Professor Calculus.

Ships shown which are identifiable, though not named

In *Land of Black Gold* the Thom(p)sons embark in sailor dress with hats bearing the name 'Titanic'

Léopoldville II
(Tintin in the Congo)
A steamship built in 1928 by the Cockerill company at Hoboken, belonging to the Maritime Company of Antwerp. Refurbished in 1937. Capable of transporting 362 passengers at an average speed of 15 knots. Before the war she sailed the route between Antwerp and the Belgian Congo. For the 1946 colour edition of *Tintin in the Congo*, Hergé copied a photograph of the liner. It was perhaps something of a tribute to the *'Léo'*, which was no more, having been torpedoed by a German submarine between Southampton and Cherbourg on Christmas Eve 1944 while carrying more than 2,000 American troops.

Normandie
(Tintin in America)
Built at Saint-Nazaire and launched in 1935, some three years after Tintin completed his American adventure in the original black-and-white edition. In the 1946 colour edition, Tintin takes the liner back to Europe. Curiously, no smoke is seen escaping from the ship's three funnels as she steams out to sea.

Prince Baudouin
(The Black Island)
The Ostend-Dover ferry on which Tintin crosses the Channel. Named after the young Belgian prince and future king. With a magnifying glass, the name is just discernible on the bow in the first black-and-white edition of 1938. It is dropped in the later colour editions.

Sirius
(The Secret of the Unicorn)
A small painting of this celebrated English cross-Channel steamer, which became the first to traverse the Atlantic entirely under steam, hangs to the left of the portrait of Haddock's illustrious ancestor, Sir Francis Haddock, in the captain's flat. In 1838 the *Sirius* took 18 days and 10 hours to cross the Atlantic between Cork and New York at an average speed of 6.7 knots.

EARLY EDITIONS IN BLACK AND WHITE

SHIPS MENTIONED AND SHOWN

The **DJEBEL AMILAH**, **HARIKA MARU** (carrying opium to Marseilles – a detail dropped in the later colour edition), **KARABOUDJAN, RANCHI, VILLE DE LYON** and **WASHINGTON** all feature in the early (pre-war) black-and-white editions. So do the following vessels:

CITY OF DOODLECASTLE
(Cigars of the Pharaoh)
This vessel resembling a tugboat is the predecessor to the **SERENO** of the colour editions. She is carrying a cargo of opium declared as 'cocoa'. The name of her captain is not given, though it is not Allan Thompson. He jettisons the coffins – containing Tintin, Snowy and Professor Sarcophagus – into the sea because he is not interested in 'antiques'. He then slips away discreetly without being disturbed by any coastguard patrol. The early edition of *The Blue Lotus* reveals that the **CITY OF DOODLECASTLE**, which is one of a number of ships operated by the villainous Mitsuhirato, has a load of opium destined for Antwerp.

PRINCE BAUDOUIN
(The Black Island)
The ferry's name is just visible under magnification. She sails between Ostend and Dover, and flies the Belgian flag.

RAMPURA
(The Blue Lotus)
The liner on which Tintin sails from Shanghai to Belgium via Hong Kong, Singapore, Colombo, Bombay, Aden, Port Said, Malta, Marseilles, Gibraltar and Southampton. It is the same ship as the **RANCHI** in the colour edition, but bears the name of another town in northern India.

THYSVILLE
(Tintin in the Congo)
The liner on which Tintin embarks for his African adventure is modelled on an actual twin-propeller ship which took her name from the town in the Belgian Congo named after Albert Thys (1849-1915), founder of the Congo Company for Trade and Industry. Today the town is called Songololo. This liner – or more exactly mixed-cargo vessel – was 500 feet long and weighed 8,200 tons. She was built by the Cockerill concern at Hoboken, and was launched in 1922, serving the line linking Antwerp with the Congo. She was sold by the Belgian Maritime Company during the 1950s.

SHIPS MENTIONED BUT NOT SHOWN

The ships **BENARES**, **JUPITER** and **TANGANYIKA** are already mentioned in the early black-and-white editions. To these can be added the **VILLE DE ROUEN**, part of Mitsuhirato's fleet and carrying opium to Le Havre in the original French version of *The Blue Lotus*. Mitsuhirato is operating six vessels, but – as in the later colour edition, though with different names – only three names are legible on his wall chart: **HARIKA MARU**, **CITY OF DOODLECASTLE** and **VILLE DE ROUEN**. The **VILLE DE ROUEN** is also mentioned in the French version of *The Shooting Star*.

SHIPS SHOWN WHICH ARE IDENTIFIABLE, THOUGH NOT NAMED

The **NORMANDIE** is the only ship to fall into this category. She features at the end of *The Broken Ear*. The black-and-white edition specifies that 'Two weeks later, Tintin returned to Europe', and under this caption appears the majestic form of the **NORMANDIE**, which for the past two years had been sailing the route Le Havre-Southampton-New York. Hergé does, however, make the mistake of having smoke pour from all three funnels, when in fact the third funnel was non-functional and there solely for aesthetic reasons.

SUPPLEMENT AU «VINGTIEME SIECLE» DU Jeudi 27 octobre 1932 N. 43

le petit vingtième

THE NAME 'HADDOCK'

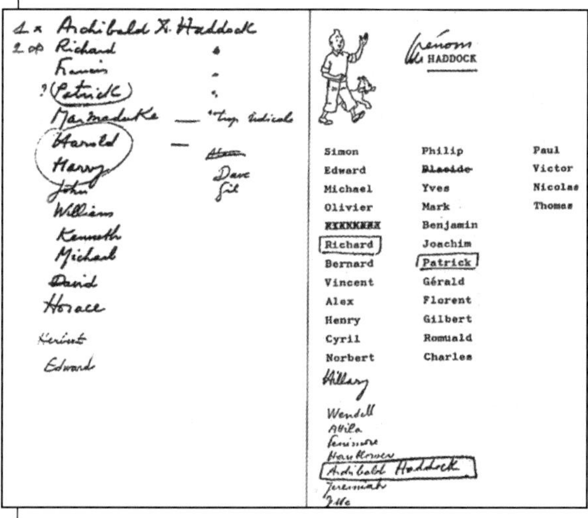

When asked by journalists who was behind Captain Haddock, Hergé always maintained that a particular model did not exist.

Notes for *Tintin and the Picaros*: Hergé makes a list of possible first names for the captain

The name, unlike those chosen for Professor Calculus and Jolyon Wagg, was not one he had to seek. 'Haddock ... just came like that,' he said later.

'It's very difficult to be precise about such things, because they generally happen subconsciously,' Hergé told a radio interviewer in 1977. There are a number of theories about what might have prompted the name.

In the original French version, an inebriated Captain Haddock sings an instantly recognizable line from a popular film musical, *Captain Craddock*, which was made in 1933. Hergé was an avid cinema-goer.

Others have suggested a literary antecedent in Jules Verne's *L'Île mystérieuse (The Mysterious Island)*, where the sailor Pencroff is also bearded, irascible, an inveterate pipe-smoker and a master of invective.

Hergé acknowledged that with all his characters he adopted here and there certain characteristics he found in his friends or in people he came across. 'As for example with Captain Haddock: in part he's my friend the cartoonist [Edgar-Pierre] Jacobs, who like him is gruff, who is capable of expansive gestures and prone occasionally to little mishaps.'

Captain Haddock's first name, Archibald, is revealed only in the final completed Tintin adventure, *Tintin and the Picaros*, published in 1976. Notes that Hergé kept at the time he was working on the book show a long list of predominantly Anglo-Saxon names he considered for the captain, with the palpably Scottish Archibald emerging as the first choice after much deliberation. It clearly confirms the captain's British ancestry.

Whatever the origins of the name, when working on *The Crab with the Golden Claws* in 1940 Hergé had no idea what the future held in store for his newly created character.

THUNDERING TYPHOONS!

Hergé's English translators, Leslie Lonsdale Cooper and Michael Turner, in one of the many moments of inspiration came up wit this memorable expletive for the 'Tonnerr de Brest!' so explosively and regularl exclaimed by Haddock. 'Blistering barnacle is their equally successful alternative to hi 'Mille sabords!' in French.

The French 'Tonnerre de Brest' would seen to be inspired by the famous cannon at Bres Prison, which from the mid-eighteent century was fired – with a report like a thun derclap – whenever a prisoner escaped. Th local populace would then take arms an endeavour to capture the convict and claim reward.

Hergé picked up the expression from hi friend the art-gallery director Marcel Sta Hergé was a regular visitor at Stal's Carrefou Gallery in Brussels.

THE HISTORY OF SIR FRANCIS HADDOCK

In the original French version of* The Secret of the Unicorn, *Captain Haddock identifies his illustrious seventeenth-century ancestor, whose portrait hangs in his flat, as François, Chevalier de Hadoque, a doughty sea captain serving in the navy of Louis XIV, the Sun King.
In the reconstructed document which Professor Calculus shows Tintin towards the end of* Red Rackham's Treasure, *Louis declares that for his services to the Crown the chevalier is to be rewarded with the château of Moulinsart.

Historically, this transforms comfortably for the English edition, which, published in 1959, was one of the first Tintin adventures to appear in English. The chevalier becomes even more convincingly Sir Francis Haddock, serving in the navy of Charles II. The fragmentary document produced at the end of *Red Rackham's Treasure* states, 'Charles the Second, by ye Grace of God King of England, desiring to reward Our trusty and beloved Knight, Francis Haddock, Lieutenant in Our Navy for his devoted service, Doth hereby grant and bestow Our ... manor of Marlinspike, Messuages and tenements ... ' The document is dated July 1677.

In the French edition, Louis XIV, who reigned from 1643 to 1715, issues the document seven years later, in 1684. Charles II, who had returned from exile on the restoration of the monarchy in 1660, died in 1685.

'Marlinspike' is the suitably nautical-sounding English name devised by Turner and Lonsdale-Cooper as a substitute for 'Moulinsart'.

'Haddock', as Hergé knew, was a splendid name for a sea captain, and ever since Queen Elizabeth I knighted Drake on the deck of the *Golden Hind*, in 1580, 'Sir Francis' has had a special nautical resonance. We can add to it from recent times the name of Sir Francis Chichester, whose yacht *Gypsy Moth* has become one of the sights of Greenwich.

Most remarkable, however, was Hergé's discovery some years later that there was in England a family by the name of Haddock with a distinguished naval pedigree, producing two admirals and at least a dozen captains in the seventeenth and eighteenth centuries, including Sir Richard Haddock, a direct contemporary of Sir Francis.

Hergé was astounded. 'An extraordinary coincidence,' he declared; 'needless to say I was unaware of this when I created Captain Haddock.'

Red Rackham, the pirate chief who against the odds vanquishes Sir Francis Haddock in 1676, is not an entirely fictional character. His names were derived from those of two actual buccaneers: the Englishman John Rackham, operating around 1720, and the Haitian pirate Lerouge, active in 1814.

His extravagant attire is based on that of a third pirate, called Montbars, who inspired terror around 1650. Hergé added a distinctive, grinning, tooth-dominated visage and credited Rackham with the incredible feat of overcoming a 50-cannon warship.

In the original French versions of *The Secret of the Unicorn* and *Red Rackham's Treasure*, the Chevalier de Hadoque, despite his name, seems to have English roots.

It has even been suggested that he was an English sea captain who had served the Stuarts in the Royal Navy and then, as a Jacobite, had switched to Louis XIV's fleet, allowing the name 'Haddock' to be adapted to the French-sounding 'Hadoque'. As a similar example, it is pointed out that in diplomatic dispatches the Duke of Buckingham was addressed in French as 'Monsieur de Bouquinquant'.

This theory is, however, problematic when it comes to dates, for the chevalier is named as a lieutenant in the navy of Louis XIV in 1684, four years before the Stuarts lost the monarchy with the departure of James II and his followers for exile in France and the accession of William and Mary to the throne.

A more plausible explanation could be that, in the wake of the English Civil War, Sir Francis's father – himself a naval officer, a royalist, and possibly a Catholic – fled to a French exile in 1650. His son allowed the family name to be modified to 'Hadoque' and served in the French navy all too aware of the traditions of the Royal Navy on account of his father.

There are a number of indications that the chevalier spoke English and was familiar with Royal Navy customs:

1 - The question of rum. In the French navy of the seventeenth century it would never have occurred to a sailor to drink rum, which was an English custom. But, the moment he has freed himself from his shackles, the chevalier grabs a bottle of rum. Where did he acquire such habits, if not from his English background?

2 - The cannon on the *Unicorn* are secured in the English manner and in fact are reminiscent of those on Nelson's *Victory*. Certainly the arrangement suggests a familiarity with English naval artillery.

3 - When the *Unicorn*, from which the chevalier has just slipped away, blows up, he stands up in the jolly-boat and cries, 'Hurrah! Justice is done!' The shout of 'Hurrah!', which much later became the obligatory greeting for visiting heads of state or government on boarding French warships, would have been unheard of in the navy of Louis XIV, though it would have been familiar in the Royal Navy.

4 - On the parchments giving the bearings of the chevalier's island, W is used to denote west, whereas at that time west was always O to French navigators – for 'Ouest'. The English, of course, used W for west.

An engraving depicting John Rackham

The historic Rackham

At the beginning of the eighteenth century a pirate called John Rackham was the scourge of the Caribbean. The writer Daniel Defoe refers to him. Also known as Calico Jack, on account of his brightly coloured cotton clothes, Rackham was the boatswain on the *Dragon*, an English vessel based in the Bahamas. If one re-creates the naval engagement north-west of Haiti in which the *Unicorn* is overcome, it is evident that Red Rackham's vessel is indeed coming from the Bahamas.

The real Rackham later headed a mutiny that toppled the *Dragon*'s captain, Charley Vane, who according to one account was marooned on a desert island, or, according to another, was put adrift on a sloop with some loyal crew members.

Montbars the Exterminator – an engraving by Rascalon

THE THREE RACKHAMS

The *Dragon*, now under Rackham's command, continued to terrorize Caribbean waters, depositing her booty on a deserted island of the Bahamas. An account dating from 1719 tells of Rackham and his crew spending Christmas on a small island where they would drink and feast until their provisions ran out.

Hergé's Red Rackham tells the captured Sir Francis of 'the booty we captured from a Spaniard three days ago'. Hergé was certainly familiar with Ludwig Bühnau's account of the real (John) Rackham's capture of an enormous Spanish ship laden with treasure, which was to lead to the pirate's downfall. To celebrate their triumph, his crew retired to a small island that was believed to be safe, to enjoy several days of hard drinking. As Haddock tells Tintin, 'Towards nightfall, the *Unicorn* with her pirate crew sighted a small island. Soon she dropped anchor in a sheltered cove ... Darkness fell; the pirates found the *Unicorn*'s cargo of rum, broached the casks, and made themselves abominably drunk ...' However, pirates also preyed on pirates, and another band of buccaneers found the narrow passage that led to the island and caught Rackham's drunken crew by surprise.

John Rackham alias Calico Jack was a young man described as 'brown-skinned with blond hair'. An engraving shows him clean-shaven and wearing a three-cornered hat.

In fact Calico Jack was an indolent type who preferred to spend much of his time in his cabin, stretched out on his bunk. His successes remained modest. During two years of combing the Caribbean he captured twenty ships, the majority of which were fishing vessels or small coasters. One day he could claim from a schooner no more than '50 twists of tobacco and nine bags of peppers'.

Finally he was captured, and on 28 November 1720 he was hanged in Jamaica.

Lerouge

The Haitian pirate Lerouge (The Red) was active in the Caribbean in 1814 and features in a novel, *The Corsair from Connecticut*, by C. S. Forester, best known for the Hornblower books and a master of maritime narrative. Whether out of bravado or in allusion to his name, Lerouge habitually wore a red tunic that he had stolen from the baggage of a British officer. His schooner, the *Susannah*, was boarded and captured near Martinique by an American privateer and he was summarily hanged. Hergé seems to have known about the real or fictitious Lerouge, and incorporated him in his pirate creation – Red Rackham.

Montbars the Exterminator

Hergé's Red Rackham bears little visual resemblance to the real John Rackham or Calico Jack, who was a good twenty years younger. His dress is much more old-fashioned, more reminiscent of a musketeer of the reign of Louis XIII (or Charles I in England) with his flamboyant hat, cape and kidskin boots. In fact Red Rackham's outfit echoes very precisely that of another celebrated pirate, known as Montbars the Exterminator. A member of the Languedoc gentry, in the mid-seventeenth century Montbars led a band of buccaneers who eschewed rape and booty but sought revenge on the Spanish – whom they detested – for their massacres of the native Indians. Hergé used a reproduction of an engraving of Montbars by Rascalon as his model.

OUTSIDE CHARACTERS DRAWN INTO THE ADVENTURES

Three characters who feature in Hergé's adventures of Tintin at sea are based on real-life personalities.

Auguste Piccard

Professor Calculus was directly inspired by the lanky, distinctive figure of the Swiss physics professor Auguste Piccard (1884–1962). A university teaching appointment brought Piccard regularly to Brussels, where Hergé would spot his unmistakable figure in the street. Piccard had a number of scientific achievements to his credit, the most Calculus-like being his deep-water exploration submarine or bathyscaphe, with which he began experiments in 1948. 'Calculus is a reduced-scale Piccard, as the real chap was very tall,' Hergé told his interviewer Numa Sadoul. 'He had an interminable neck that sprouted from a collar that was much too large ... I made Calculus a "mini-Piccard", otherwise I would have had to enlarge the frames of the cartoon strip.'
Piccard as he was in real life is portrayed as the distinguished-looking gentleman in the long brown overcoat who, in the large plate on the final page of *Red Rackham's Treasure*, is examining the case containing Sir Francis Haddock's hat, pistol and cutlass, a couple of yards away from the Professor Calculus he inspired. With whitened hair, he is also the model for the scientist on the right of the frame at the send-off for the European Foundation for Scientific Research group in *The Shooting Star*.

Henri de Monfreid

The writer and adventurer Henri de Monfreid (1879-1974) was another colourful personality whom Hergé worked into his books. As Hergé admitted himself, 'You know that I was inspired by Henri de Monfreid not only for *The Red Sea Sharks*, but particularly in *Cigars of the Pharaoh* – he's the gun-runner who takes Tintin on board his boat on the Red Sea, which he is using for illegal arms shipments.'
This episode was directly inspired by a passage in de Monfreid's 1932 best-seller *Les Secrets de la mer Rouge (Secrets of the Red Sea)*. There is, moreover, a marked resemblance between photographs of de Monfreid at the time and the pipe-smoking sea captain depicted by Hergé, though the latter appears perhaps a few years younger in the later colour version of the adventure. In reality de Monfreid would probably have dispensed with the yachtsman's cap, taking on a somewhat more exotic appearance. He would adopt local dress and speak the language, often passing as a native.
Hergé had certainly read *Secrets of the Red Sea*. As in de Monfreid's novel, Hergé´s sea captain had a store of dynamite in the hold, so that if the worst came to the worst he could blow his boat sky high.

Lionel Crabb

Commander Lionel 'Buster' Crabb was the Royal Navy frogman and intelligence officer whose headless body was washed ashore after a bungled attempt to inspect the hull of a Soviet cruiser moored at

Auguste Piccard, on the right of the group

Southampton in 1956. A photograph of Crabb clutching a limpet mine was used for the cover of a book, *Les hommes-grenouilles* (*The Frogmen*), which appeared in 1955, when Crabb, a well-known frogman, was still alive. It was a translation of a book in German by Cajus Bekker. In *The Red Sea Sharks*, Hergé used the book cover photograph directly for his drawing of the frogman about to dive from the submarine holding a limpet mine, which he intends to plant on the hull of the *Ramona*. Every detail of the equipment and the face itself is scrupulously copied.

SNOWY ON BOARD

Snowy is to Tintin what the sea is to boats!

Snowy provides an indispensable expression of the emotions associated with adventure and friendship.

During the epoch of the great transatlantic liners, the *Queen Mary*, the *Queen Elizabeth* and the *Normandie*, special menus could be ordered for the dogs of passengers. Snowy, however, has his own ideas, preferring to pilfer the meals prepared in the galley.

Tintin's companion is greedy and waggish, but also very vulnerable. In *The Shooting Star* he symbolizes the violence of the storm, being swept helplessly towards the scupper hole and saved by Tintin only at the very last moment.

In turn, Snowy defuses traps and extricates his master from the most hopeless situations. Even if he is sometimes perplexed at Tintin's initiatives, he provides the necessary counterpoint in all the adventures. Snowy's personal characteristics are not dissimilar to Captain Haddock's. He is partial to whisky and champagne, and is torn between his greedier instincts and his sense of duty to Tintin.

While there is much in common between Snowy and Captain Haddock, it is also true that Tintin and his four-legged companion often echo each other's positions. Together on the *Aurora* they share the exhilaration of breathing in the bracing sea air; on the *Ramona* they dance the same exuberant dance of joy at their rescue.

They share the same dangers, joys and pleasures. Hergé shows them in attitudes which are so similar that to readers they become inseparable and highly engaging.

Yveline Yvernogeau

LIST OF SAILORS MENTIONED

ALONZO
A sailor on board the *Pachacamac*, named but not shown on page 8 of *Prisoners of the Sun*.

BILL
The ship's cook who enters the bar on page 1 of *Red Rackham's Treasure* and serves on the *Sirius*. Earlier, in *The Shooting Star*, he was employed on the *Aurora*.

CHESTER
An old sailing companion of Captain Haddock, who has known him for more than twenty years. They meet again at Akureyi in Iceland, where Chester is captain of the *Sirius*, a boat which he lends to Haddock for the treasure hunt in *The Secret of the Unicorn*. On page 59 of *The Seven Crystal Balls* Tintin and Haddock decide to go on to Bridgeport, where Chester is with the *Sirius*. In *The Castafiore Emerald* Chester sends a telegram to Captain Haddock congratulating him on his 'engagement'.

DAWES, HERBERT
Herbert Dawes is the sailor from the *Karaboudjan* who is found drowned in *The Crab with the Golden Claws*. He is not shown.

DIEGO THE DREADFUL
Red Rackham's mate in *The Secret of the Unicorn*, killed by Sir Francis Haddock.

FRANK
One of the officers on the *Peary* in *The Shooting Star*. Armed with a rifle with a telescopic sight, he attempts to shoot Tintin as he parachutes on to the meteorite. In the French version he is called Douglas.

GEORGE
A sailor who talks to Bill, the ship's cook, in The Anchor bar on the opening page of *Red Rackham's Treasure*.

HADDOCK, ARCHIBALD
Captain of the *Karaboudjan* in *The Crab with the Golden Claws*, where his alcoholism allows him to be subjugated by his first mate, Allan Thompson. Captains the *Aurora* in *The Shooting Star*. Descended from Sir Francis Haddock, he captains the *Sirius* – borrowed from his friend Captain Chester – in an expedition to recover *Red Rackham's Treasure*.

Shipwrecked in *The Red Sea Sharks* and picked up by the yacht *Scheherazade*, he is transferred to the *Ramona*, where he comes across Allan Thompson again.

HADDOCK, SIR FRANCIS
Ancestor of Captain Haddock. Serving in the Royal Navy of Charles II, he captains the *Unicorn*, a warship carrying 50 cannon, which he loses to the pirate Red Rackham. He flees the captured vessel with the treasure after laying an explosive charge which destroys the *Unicorn*. He then spends two years on a desert island. In the French version he is the chevalier François de Hadoque, an officer in the navy of Louis XIV.

JOE
A sailor on the *Ramona*, referred to on page 43 of *The Red Sea Sharks*.

JUMBO
A sailor on the *Karaboudjan* in *The Crab with the Golden Claws*. In the early editions he is black, but objections from the American censor on the appearance together of black and white characters in a book destined for children led to Hergé changing him in later editions into a sailor of Puerto Rican appearance.

KURT
The commander of the submarine code-named *Shark* in *The Red Sea Sharks*. His German name and the fact that his command is an old U-boat indicate that he had served in the *Kriegsmarine*.

MACGREGOR
A Kiltoch fisherman who disappears in *The Black Island*.

MCPHEE, JOCK
In *Land of Black Gold*, a sailor on the *Speedol Star* who claims to work for Naval Intelligence but is in fact a member of a gang of cocaine smugglers.

MALDEMER
Captain of the liner *Ville de Lyon* in *The Broken Ear*. His name is a pun on the French for seasickness, *mal de mer*. In the French version he has the rather splendid name of Le Goffic, while in the original black-and-white edition he is Captain Dupont. Hergé changed this, however, to prevent any confusion with Dupond and Dupont, the French names of the Thom(p)sons.

OLSSON, C.
A sailor on board the *Ramona* whose name is inscribed on a green trunk in *The Red Sea Sharks*.

PARKER
A naval officer on the *Scheherazade*, the yacht belonging to Rastapopolous, alias the Marquis di Gorgonzola, in *The Red Sea Sharks*.

PEDRO
A sailor on board the *Karaboudjan* on page 12 of *The Crab with the Golden Claws*.

RED RACKHAM
The pirate captain who in 1676 captures the *Unicorn* of Sir Francis Haddock. Sir Francis later kills him in a duel.

THOMPSON, ALLAN
First mate of the *Karaboudjan*, who bullies Captain Haddock in *The Crab with the Golden Claws*. As early as *Cigars of the Pharaoh*, where he is in charge of the yacht *Sereno*, he is in the employ of Roberto Rastapopoulos smuggling drugs. In *The Crab with the Golden Claws* he takes over command of the *Karaboudjan*, whose name is illegally altered to the *Djemel Amilah*. In *The Red Sea Sharks* he commands the *Ramona*. In *Flight 714* he takes part in the skyjacking of the jet belonging to billionaire Laszlo Carreidas.

THOMSON AND THOMPSON
The Special Branch detectives who join the *Sirius* as crew in *Red Rackham's Treasure*. They dress in full naval rig again in *Land of Black Gold* as part of the complement of the oil tanker *Speedol Star*. On this occasion their sailor hats are emblazoned with the legend 'Titanic'.

TOM
The accomplice of Allan Thompson on the *Karaboudjan* in *The Crab with the Golden Claws*.

TOM
The American sailor who operates the heliograph aboard the USS *Los Angeles* in *The Red Sea Sharks*.

HERGÉ AND CHRISTOPHER COLUMBUS

Christopher Columbus clearly made a deep impression on Hergé, who mentions him five times in *The Adventures of Tintin*.

- Thomson and Thompson in *The Black Island*: 'To quote Christopher Columbus ... er ... Captain Cook ... '
- The same pair in *King Ottokar's Sceptre*: '"Only three days," said Columbus, "and I will give you a new world!"'
- In *Prisoners of the Sun* the hotel at Callao, the Cristobal Colon, is named after the great explorer.
- In the French version of *The Castafiore Emerald*, on hearing that Bianca Castafiore is about to embark on a tour of America, Haddock observes, 'Poor Yanks! Things were so quiet before Christopher Columbus!'
- In the same adventure, again in the French version, Professor Calculus compares his invention of colour television to the inspiration of Columbus.

Hergé knew all about Columbus. In *Prisoners of the Sun* his finale using an eclipse was taken from Columbus, who in 1503 put an end to a rebellion of Jamaicans by referring to an astronomical calendar published in 1473 by Johannes Müller (Regiomontanus), to predict an eclipse.

NAVIGATION

WHERE DID THE METEORITE FALL?

Hergé left a few scattered clues which make it possible to pinpoint the location where the meteorite fell in Arctic waters in The Shooting Star.

1 Three days before discovering the small island created by the meteorite, the *Aurora* crosses the 72nd parallel and Haddock gives his orders to the seaplane pilot: 'You will confine your search to an area between 73 and 78 North, and 8 and 13 West ... You understand?'

2 The seaplane flies for exactly two hours, between 10.15 and 12.15.

3 At 12.15 the seaplane sights a column of white vapour rising from the sea – caused by the meteorite – 'from one spot about 20° East'.

The cruising speed of an aircraft of this type would be about 120 m.p.h. It is therefore certain that the seaplane, at the time it locates the column of vapour, is itself between 77° and 78° degrees of latitude north.

What is the longitude? 'Between ... 8 and 13 West,' the captain instructed, but his pencil on the map indicates 9° west, which suggests that the seaplane has flown north by 9° west with the intention of descending through 12° to sweep the area between 8° and 13° west.

The meteorite is therefore to be found on an oblique stretch, one degree of latitude (60 nautical miles) wide, forming an angle of 20° with 9° west.

Hergé has also given us three other pieces of information from which to determine the geographical coordinates, stemming this time from the navigation of the rival ship, the *Peary*.

4 Three days before the discovery of the meteorite, between 12.30 and 13.00 hours, the *Peary* is to be found at 12° 23' W and 76° 40' N.

5 She is travelling at a supposedly constant speed of 12 knots.

6 From the time of giving her position until she stops before the meteorite, on discovery day at 10.00 hours, the *Peary* has covered some 540 nautical miles (45 hours at 12 knots).

The meteorite is therefore to be found on the arc of a circle whose centre is at 12° 23' W and 76° 40' N and whose radius is 540 nautical miles. The intersection between this arc of the circle and the stretch outlined above gives a small arc 60 nautical miles long midway between Spitsbergen and the North Pole where the small island formed by the meteorite sinks into the sea.

Further refining the available information, taking into account the seaplane's position of departure, the time needed for its catapult launch, landing and recovery, the extent of the detour needed for the identification of the Peary, and the additional indication given by Captain Haddock in the French version when he orders the coxswain at the wheel 'to steer North by 12° East' following the return of the seaplane, it is possible, with a margin of error of not more than 10 per cent, to pinpoint the meteorite's position at 84° north, 20° east.

It is the same latitude as Cape Morris, where the seal-hunters saw a fireball cross the sky and disappear over the horizon.

Meanwhile
R.S. Peary, 12°23'W., 76° 40' N., to Bohlwinkel, Sao Rico. Have been spotted by E.F.S.R. aircraft. Presume Aurora in vicinity. We are putting on steam.
4

6

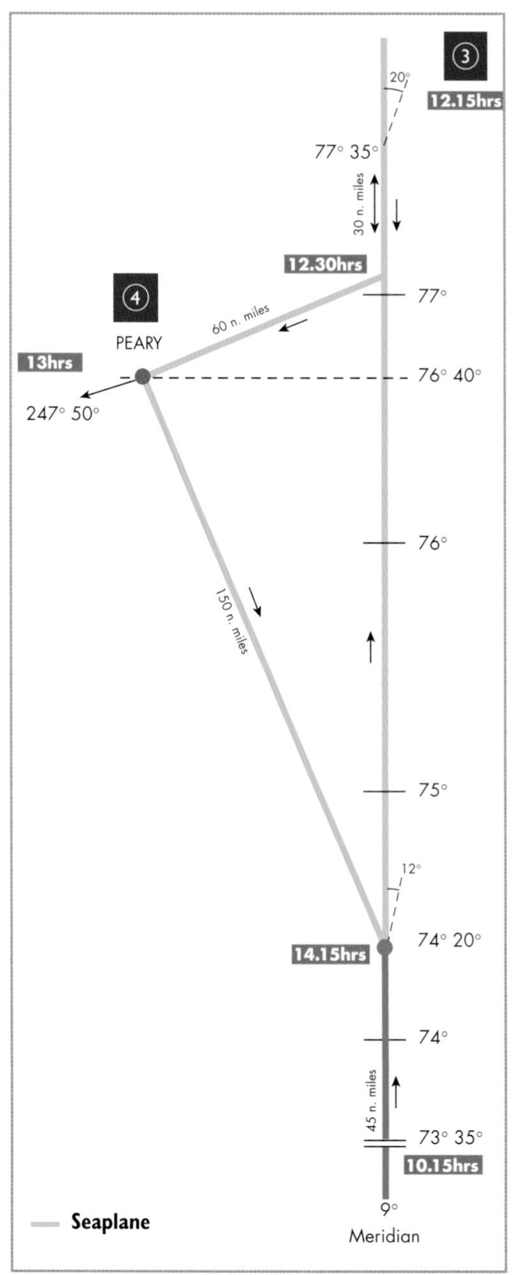
3
20°
12.15hrs
77° 35°
30 n. miles
12.30hrs
77°
4
PEARY
60 n. miles
13hrs
76° 40°
247° 50°
76°
150 n. miles
75°
12°
14.15hrs
74° 20°
74°
45 n. miles
73° 35°
10.15hrs
9°
Meridian
Seaplane

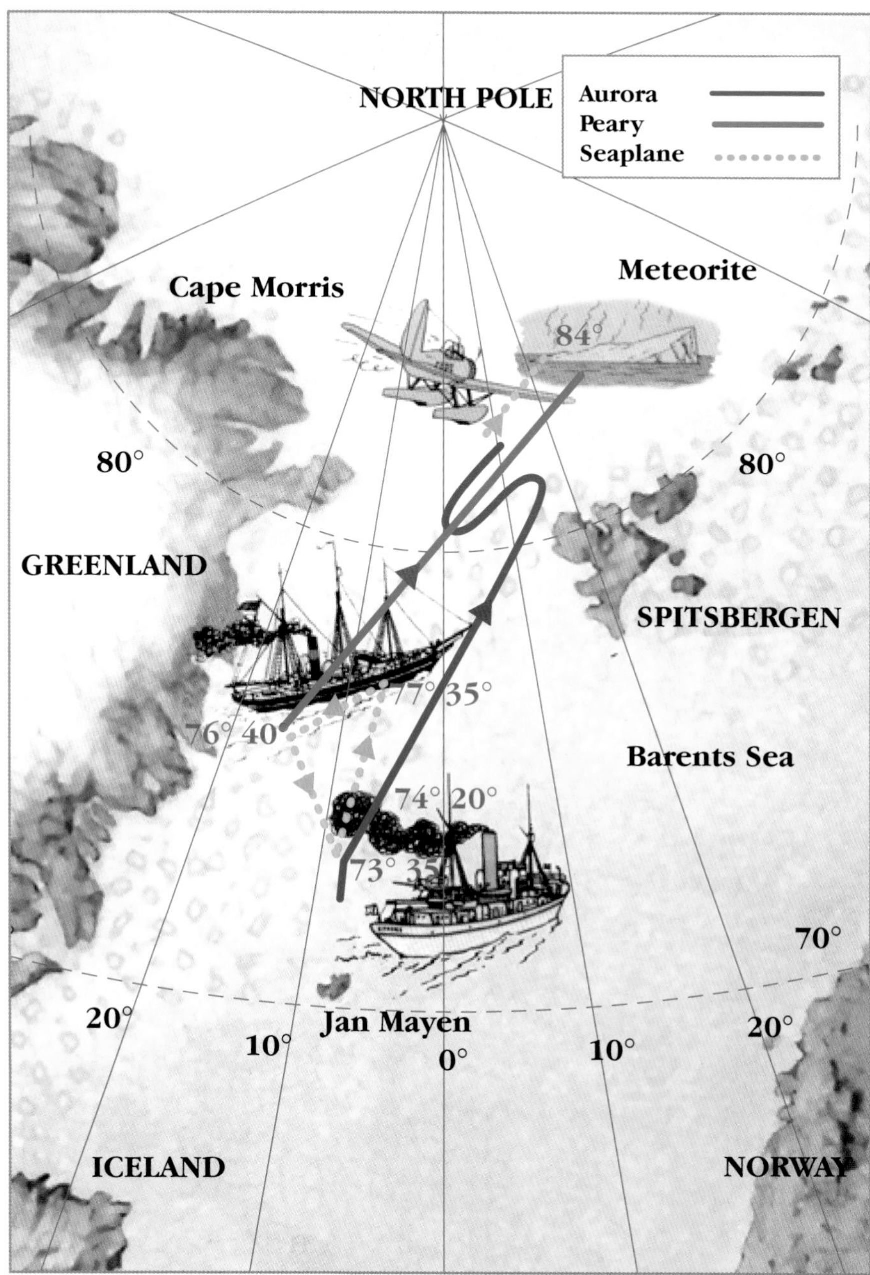
NORTH POLE
Aurora
Peary
Seaplane
Cape Morris
Meteorite
84°
80°
80°
GREENLAND
SPITSBERGEN
77° 35°
76° 40
Barents Sea
74° 20°
73° 35
70°
20°
10°
Jan Mayen
0°
10°
20°
ICELAND
NORWAY

THE LAST BATTLE OF THE UNICORN

The Unicorn fought her last battle on 24 May 1676.

The exact date does not feature in the Tintin adventure, though we know the year from the journal of Sir Francis Haddock that Captain Haddock has just read on page 14 of* The Secret of the Unicorn*. We know too that the battle occurred on the eve of a full moon and during the summer, as in those days one did not sail between October and March.

Furthermore, as Jean-Claude Lemineur has noted in his study on the *Unicorn*, on account of the frequent hurricanes in the region it was customary in the seventeenth century to suspend ship movements as much as possible between mid-July and mid-October.

Astronomical charts give the dates of full moons as 24 May and 23 June; the months of April and September are ruled out because they coincide with eclipses.

To be sure, it would be sufficient to read the calendar cross that Sir Francis has erected on his desert island and look for the day of the week when he began his sojourn. Tintin explains the meaning of the notches on the cross to Captain Haddock: 'A calendar! When your ancestor was marooned – like Robinson Crusoe, he counted the days until he was rescued. Look: there's a small notch for weekdays and a large one for Sundays ...'

There are two complete pictures of the cross on the pages of the adventure. They do not show it from the same angle, as is demonstrated by the differing gaps between the cross and the two trees. The proposition here is that in the second picture the column underneath the horizontal bar, separate from and higher than the other notches, marks the beginning of Sir Francis's time on the desert island. This column is made up of seven or eight notches (the lowest is too small to be of significance), but none corresponding to a Sunday. If we count seven markings, based on the

week that follows and begins with a Monday, it would confirm that the first day spent on the island was also a Monday. The combat the day before would therefore have been on a Sunday; however, this is not compatible with the date of a full moon. But counting eight notches, the first would be a Sunday and explicable if he had not yet had the idea of making a distinctive notch for Sundays. This would tally with the date for a full moon, and the battle would therefore have fallen on the Saturday, 24 May 1676.

As for the battle itself, we depend on Jean-Claude Lemineur for much of the interpretation that follows.

'It is the year 1676. The *Unicorn*, a valiant ship of King Charles II's fleet, has left Barbados in the West Indies, and set sail for home,' Captain Haddock recounts to Tintin. 'Two days at sea, a good stiff breeze, and the *Unicorn* is reaching on the starboard tack.' She is sailing for Europe, heading towards Florida to pick up the prevailing westerly winds which, together with the Gulf Stream, will propel her towards the old continent. Leaving St Domingo, she benefits from winds that move progressively from east to north, and then gradually to the west. Suddenly the look-out cries, 'Sail on the port bow!'

I - Sir Francis raises his telescope. 'Thundering typhoons! ... She's mighty close-hauled! Ration my rum if she's not going to cut across our bows!'

'And she's making a spanking pace! Oho! She's running up her colours ... Now we'll see ... ' And there is the pirate flag, the skull and crossbones, the Jolly Roger, flying from the mainmast of a two-masted brigantine with no guns. The ship's name is not disclosed, though we learn soon enough that of her captain, Red Rackham.

Captain Haddock takes up the tale: 'Turning on to the wind with all sails set, risking her masts, the *Unicorn* tries to outsail the dreaded Barbary buccaneers ... '

To a naval historian the most extraordinary thing is that Sir Francis, in command of a 50-cannon warship, carrying a crew of some 250 men, should try to outsail a pirate vessel manned by a few dozen buccaneers without cannon. In normal circumstances one would expect it to be the other way round: the pirate ship would make haste to escape such a powerful opponent, for fear of being blasted out of the water.

Pirates would never take on warships front on, because of the obvious disproportion of forces. Their usual tactic was to

>

HOW THE GREENWICH MERIDIAN MISLED HADDOCK

Captain Haddock was deeply disappointed when he brought the *Sirius* successfully to latitude 20° 37' 42" north, longitude 70° 52' 15" west, but failed to find the island described by his ancestor, Sir Francis Haddock. He was using the coordinates revealed in the three scraps of parchment left by Sir Francis, and understandably he took the Greenwich meridian as his starting point. It is Tintin who solves the problem: 'Well, the meridian from which you calculated the degrees of longitude was of course the Greenwich meridian ... '

'You don't suppose I used one in Timbuctoo!' replies Haddock.

'No, wait. Supposing Sir Francis Haddock used a French chart – he could easily have done. Then zero would be on the Paris meridian – and that lies more than two degrees east of Greenwich!'

'Blistering barnacles, that's an idea! You may be right! Perhaps we are too far to the west. We'll go back on our tracks ... '

They do, and later that evening they find the island.

Tintin has a point. In the seventeenth century it would have been usual to calculate longitude based on the Paris meridian, which was widely used until just before the First World War. As a result of this misunderstanding the *Sirius* steams too far west, and it is necessary to backtrack and make up the more than two degrees that separate the ancient from the modern meridian.

However, Sir Francis could well have used the 'first meridian' drawn through the Canary Isles, which dated from the ancient Egyptians and was still in use during the seventeenth century. This would have placed the island somewhere in the Gulf of Mexico!

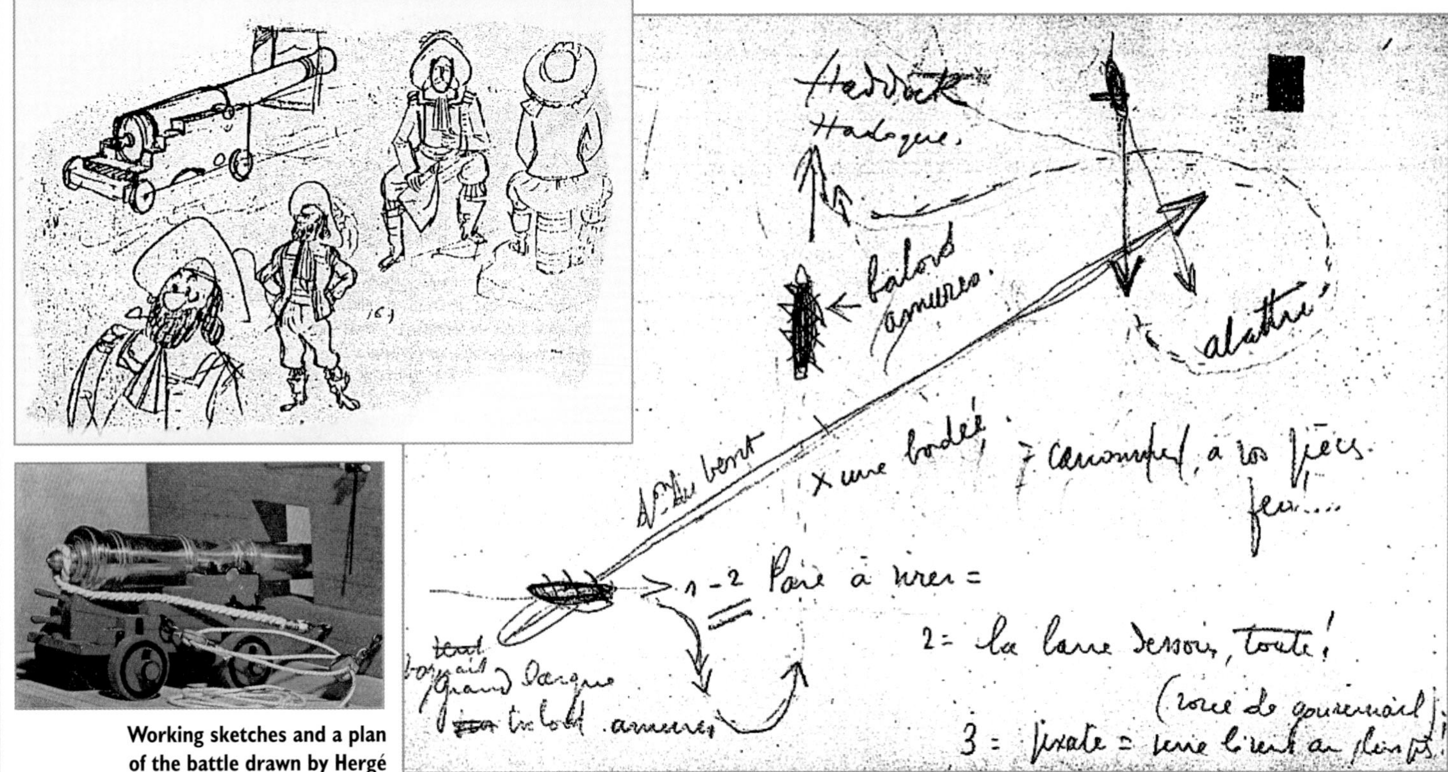

Working sketches and a plan of the battle drawn by Hergé

take money and merchandise from undefended merchant vessels or defenceless coastal regions.

Despite this anomaly, Hergé carried out his usual research on the naval battle manoeuvres he envisaged. A sketchbook exists showing a precise plan of the phases of battle and the wind direction. There is also a sketch of a cannon and of a figure similar to Sir Francis in several poses.

In Hergé's archives there are also photographs of a cannon, which might well have belonged to HMS *Victory*, Nelson's flagship preserved at Portsmouth, and of pistols and cutlasses of the period.

Having identified the pirate ship, instead of steadily maintaining his course Sir Francis strikes to starboard, turning on to the wind at an angle of about 60° and steering a course south-east-east. The brigantine immediately follows the manoeuvre, but is downwind from the *Unicorn* by about two maritime leagues (six nautical miles). Bearing in mind the distance and the parallel routes, it is unlikely that the brigantine could have closed with the *Unicorn* so quickly.

Nevertheless, Sir Francis declares, 'Thundering typhoons! It's no use ... She's overhauling us fast!'

2 - In Hergé's presentation, it takes no time for the brigantine to catch up, but there is, of course, a condensing of time between the frames. A whole range of preparations for combat have to be gone through: decks have to be cleared, hammocks have to be unslung, the cannon have to be unshackled and positioned, the gun hatches have to be opened, cannon balls and powder have to be brought up, as well as water and sand; men have to be assembled and orders given.

Captain Haddock continues his account to Tintin: 'They must outwit the pirates. The Captain makes a daring plan. He'll wear ship, then pay off on the port tack. As the *Unicorn* comes abreast of the pirate he'll loose off a broadside ... No sooner said than done! ...'

This is the best option left to Sir Francis – hard to port, as if to cut off his adversary and then to blast him with his guns. The smoke from the cannonade would envelop the brigantine, masking the manoeuvres of the *Unicorn*, which could then resume her initial course or complete tacking.

'The *Unicorn* has gybed completely round. Taken by surprise, the pirates have no time to alter course,' Captain Haddock tells Tintin. 'The royal ship bears down upon them ... Steady ...' Sir Francis then gives the command: 'Fire!'

3 - Firing into the wind at the enemy is not necessarily straightforward: the list impedes the recoil of the guns, the smoke may not clear easily, and, if the swell is heavy, it may not be possible to open the gun hatches of the lowest battery. But, as it happens, the manoeuvre was judicious: the sea was calm and the warship was higher in the water than the brigantine, giving her a more favourable angle of fire.

Withstanding a broadside of 25 cannon is not to be taken lightly, involving an avalanche of 150 kilograms battering the target. Despite this, the pirate vessel seems scarcely inconvenienced, apart from a peppering of holes in her sails and woodwork.

'Got her!' declares Sir Francis, but as his ancestor recounts, 'Got her, yes! But not a crippling blow. The pirate ship in turn goes about – and look! She's hoisted fresh colours to the mast-head!'

Furious, Red Rackham has raised the red pennant, the pirate signal for combat without mercy. As Haddock explains, 'The red pennant! ... No quarter given! ... A fight to the death, no prisoners taken! You under-

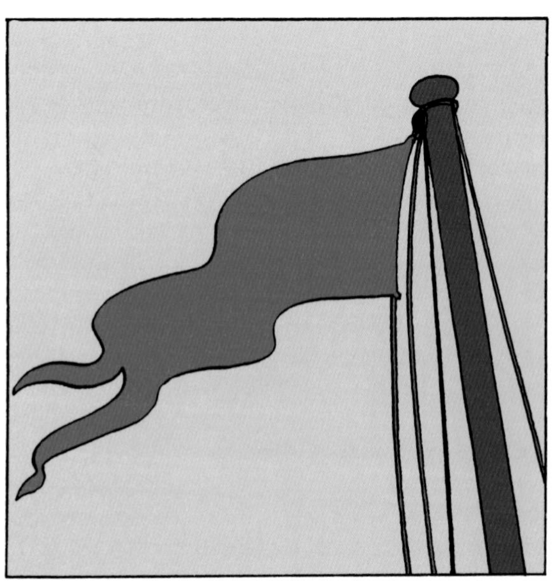

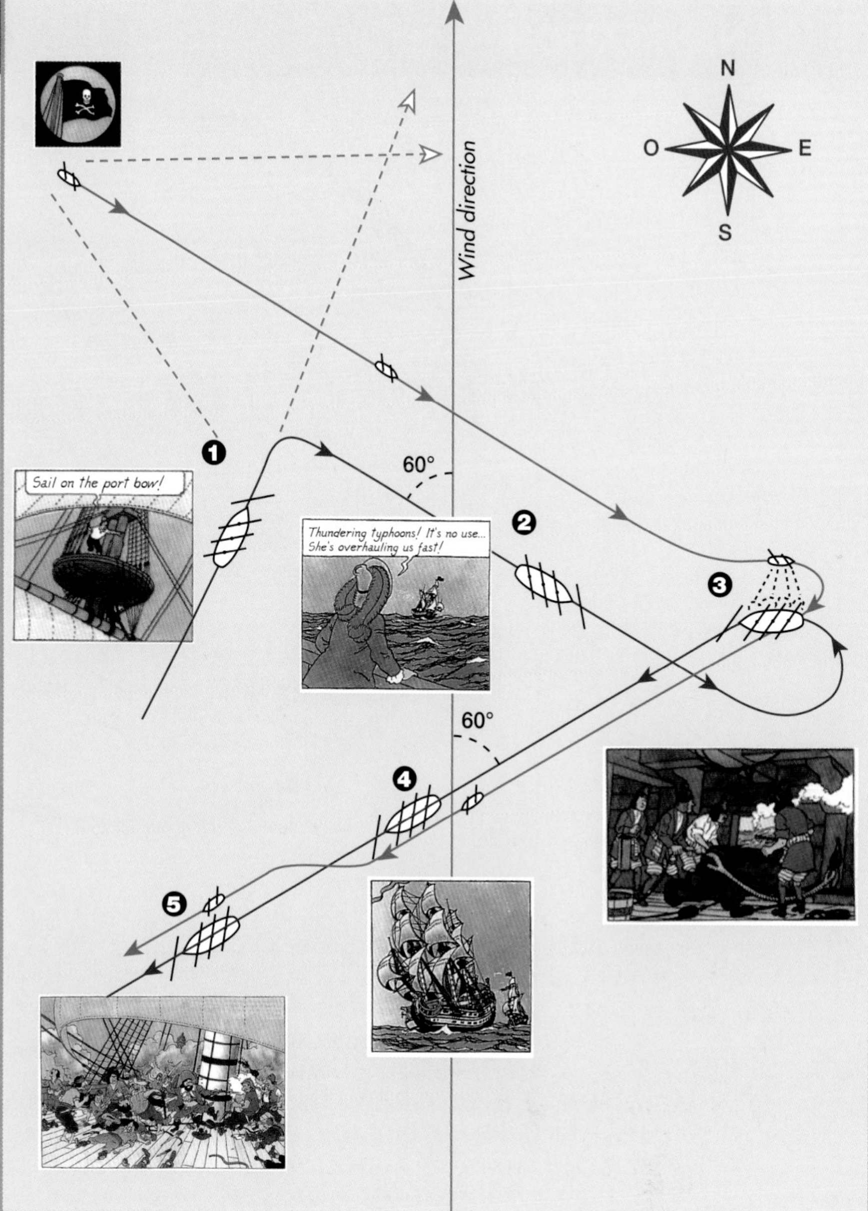

stand? If we're beaten, then it's every man to Davy Jones's locker!'

4 - The chase is resumed. The *Unicorn* continues to close to the wind on a course of south-west-west. The brigantine follows rapidly in her wake, keeping slightly to port, in the blind angle of the *Unicorn*'s guns. 'The pirates take up the chase – they draw closer ... and closer ...' Haddock continues. 'Close hauled, the enemy falls in line astern with *Unicorn*, avoiding the fire of her guns ... She draws closer.'

5 - The pirate ship catches up and, in Captain Haddock's words, 'Then suddenly, not more than half a cable's length away, she slips from under the *Unicorn*'s poop ... whoosh, like that! Then she resumes her course. The two ships are now alongside. The boarders prepare for action ... '

But, to take advantage of such a skilfully executed manoeuvre, Rackham should board the poop of the *Unicorn* where cannon are almost non-existent. To board either side of the warship verges on the suicidal, on account of the batteries, and makes a nonsense of his tactics of having kept in the blind angle of the guns during the pursuit.

Captain Haddock gives Tintin a gripping account of the final attack: 'Here they come! Grappling irons are hurled from the enemy ship. With hideous yells the pirates stream aboard the *Unicorn*.'

The scenes of boarding and the battle on the deck have to do more with Hergé's compelling drawing of narrative than with historical accuracy. Sir Francis has unexpectedly left the poop to fight at the foot of the main-mast, while a cloud of smoke masks the superstructure of the stern. There is no sign of the marine infantry – numbering at least twenty musketeers – which would form part of the company on a ship such as the *Unicorn*.

The combat itself raises a few questions. After the battle, Rackham tells Sir Francis that more than half his crew are dead or wounded. One can count 13, apart from Rackham himself, which means he would have had a crew of perhaps 30 to 40 men before the engagement. Yet Sir Francis would have commanded some 250 men – an advantage of six or seven to one.

Hergé, who hated violence, glosses over the tremendous carnage there must have been, with no quarter given. The dead and wounded in his drawings seem to be more under the influence of a general anaesthetic than victims of a violent attack. The dispatch of all Sir Francis's crew makes it easier, of course, for him to decide later to blow up his ship with the pirates on board.

Had Sir Francis not destroyed the *Unicorn*, one wonders how Rackham's surviving crew of about a dozen pirates would have managed to sail a ship normally manned by so many more.

After the battle, with Sir Francis a prisoner tied to the mast, Rackham tells him, 'My ship is foundering, damaged by your first attack, then holed below the waterline as we boarded you ... when some of your dastardly gunners fired at point blank range. She's sinking ... so my men are transferring to this ship the booty we captured from a Spaniard three days ago.'

Having transferred their booty to the *Unicorn*, the pirates sail on until the evening. Haddock tells Tintin, 'Towards nightfall, the *Unicorn* with her pirate crew sighted a small island. Soon she dropped anchor in a sheltered cove.' If the engagement took place during the morning, one would estimate that the *Unicorn* sailed on for about eight hours in pirate hands before dropping anchor that evening. She would have covered a distance of over 50 nautical miles. Since we know the bearings of the desert island from the pieces of parchment recovered by Tintin and Haddock, we can therefore place the *Unicorn*'s last battle in the waters between Haiti and Turks Island.

NAVIGATION IN THE RED SEA

The confined waters of the Red Sea are buzzing with activity in Hergé's adventure about a modern-day slave trade.

Map of the area showing distances and the sequence of action, drawn by Hergé as a guide for his use.

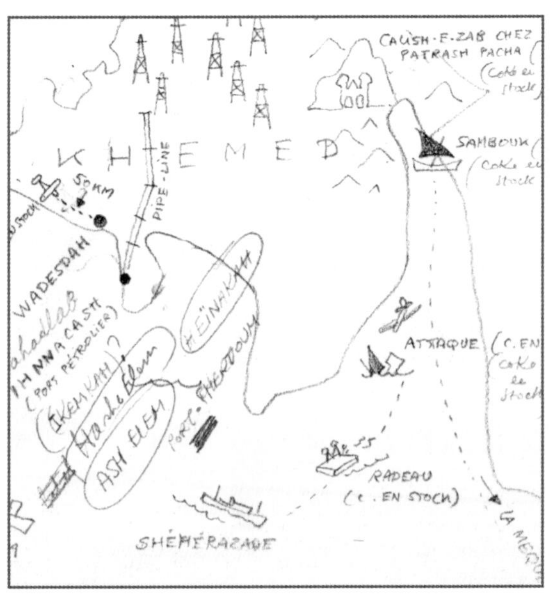

In *The Red Sea Sharks*, a total of fifteen boats and aircraft ply the waters of the Red Sea: in order of scale, the battlecruiser USS *Los Angeles*, the cargo ship *Ramona*, the yacht *Scheherazade*, two submarines, two sambuks, a launch, Allan Thompson's lifeboat, a rowing boat and a raft, as well as four aircraft.

The deployment of all these could not be left to chance, so Hergé with the help of Bob De Moor drew up a map of the area showing the positions of some of the participants and the action.

The development of the adventure also required a calendar and a timetable, which is reflected in some of the indications in the plates: 'Three days later ... ', 'Next day, at dawn ... ' or 'Half an hour later ... ' Combining such data with the actual geographical distances, and assuming that in the tropics the sun rises at 06.00 and sets at 18.00 hours, it is possible to recreate, albeit approximately, the theatre of operations and the timing of events as they unfold.

Everything begins with the rescue from the Red Sea of Tintin, Snowy and Haddock on 28 October. Why October? The newspaper article shown on page 14 of the adventure tells us in the French version that the *coup d'état* took place at Khemed on the 15th. But of which month? It must be October, because it follows the letter of 26 September addressed to General Alcazar on page 3 of the French version. Thus Tintin, Snowy and Haddock, who land at Khemed on the 19th, spend from the 22nd to the 26th at the emir's hideout, trek on horseback across the desert until dawn on the 28th, then board a sambuk on which they spend part of the morning until they are machine-gunned by a rebel Mosquito fighter-bomber. The sambuk is set on fire, and Tintin, Snowy and Haddock end up on a raft on which they are joined by Skut, the pilot of the Mosquito shot down by Tintin.

Thanks to Tintin's mirror signals, they are seen drifting and are picked up by the *Scheherazade*, the luxury yacht owned by Rastapopoulos, alias the Marquis di Gorgonzola, which is sailing in the direction of Mecca. But, having recognized the castaways as his enemies, the Marquis is only too keen to get rid of them. He sends a radio signal ordering one of his cargoes, the *Ramona*, captained by Allan Thompson, to alter course and take them on board. From the Sudanese coast the *Ramona* has previ-

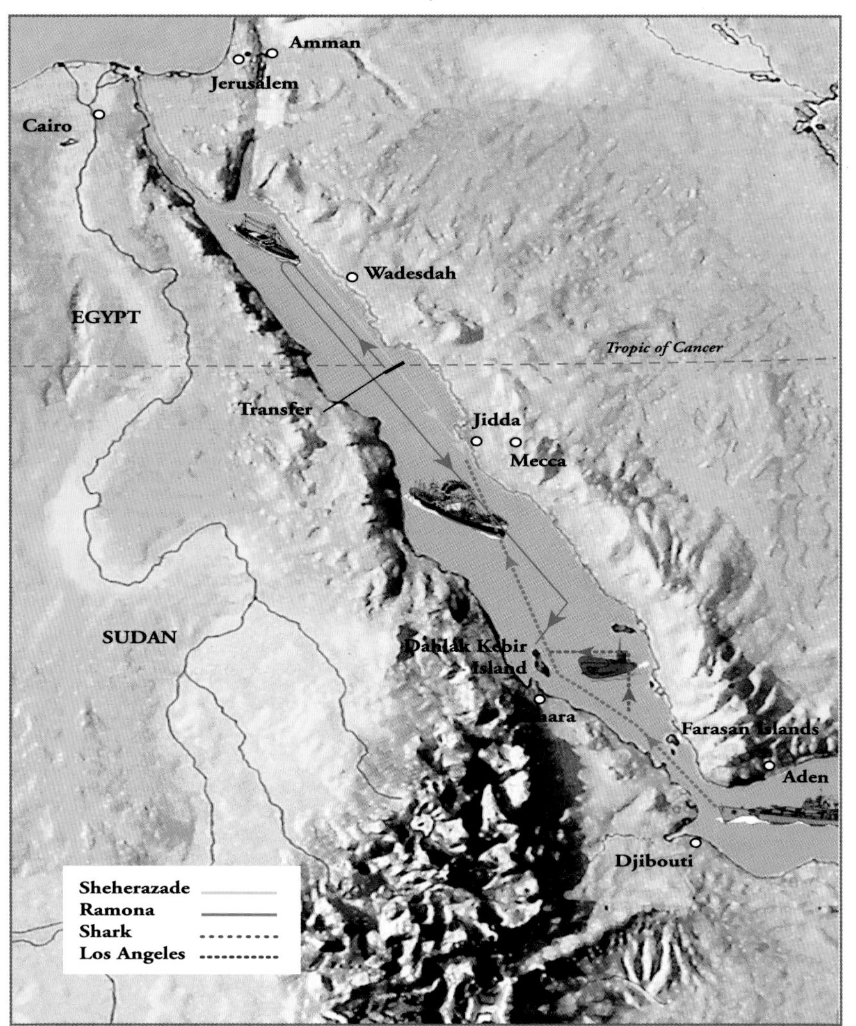

A DEBATE IN YORUBA

Contrary to what is stated by Ben Kalish Ezab on page 30 of *The Red Sea Sharks*, the pilgrims being transported aboard the *Ramona* are neither Sudanese nor Senegalese, for they speak Yoruba, a language of the south-east of Nigeria, of part of Benin and of Togo. The debate shown above is the translation into Yoruba which Hergé, in a letter dated 28 August 1957, asked a correspondent of the magazine *L'Afrique et le Monde (Africa and the World)* to provide for the following exchange:

'And me, I tell you the white man is right!'
'Yes!'
'No!'
'It's true!'

According to this letter, Hergé supposed – wrongly – that Yoruba was spoken throughout the Sudan and Mali, probably because one of his assistants charged with the translation understood 'Yoruba' on the telephone rather than 'Bambara'.

ously picked up a cargo of 'coke' – in reality black Muslims eager to make the pilgrimage to Mecca, whom it will deliver as slaves to Jidda, the port for Mecca.

So at around 05.30 hours on 29 October the castaways picked up by the *Scheherazade*

are transferred to the *Ramona* captained by Allan Thompson, who instead of proceeding to Jidda now heads northward with orders to make his vessel, the rescued castaways and the cargo of 'coke' disappear.

At 05.00 hours on 30 October, Allan Thompson sets fire to his ship – which is also loaded with ammunition – and escapes by lifeboat with his crew. The *Ramona* has by then moved some way up the Red Sea.

But, with the fire extinguished and the engines restarted by Captain Haddock, the *Ramona* resumes course for Jidda, steaming down the Red Sea at 15 knots. Towards midday she encounters the sambuk of the slave trader, who comes on board to inspect the 'merchandise'. Seen off by Haddock, the Arab leaves to make his report to Jidda while the *Ramona* changes course – steering due south – for Djibouti, as there is no longer any question of heading for Mecca. The following day – 1 November – a suspicious aeroplane flies overhead.

It radios the *Ramona*'s position – 20 miles west of the Farasan Islands steering south-south-east – to the submarine code-named *Shark*.

On Tintin's advice, Captain Haddock alters course and, instead of steaming straight for Djibouti, makes a detour of 75° to starboard. Another 3 hours and 45 minutes pass. The submarine 'steering west to intercept her' still has not sighted the *Ramona* 'a few hours later'. However, the *Shark*'s commander, Kurt, has had the good sense to carry on towards Dahlak-Kebir Island, where the spotter aeroplane relocates the *Ramona*: 'Steering due south; she is 30 miles east of Dahlak-Kebir Island.'

The duel between the cargo vessel and the submarine is about to begin. Rather than a naval engagement, the confrontation is a succession of near scrapes and mismanoeuvres to the advantage of the *Ramona*. Haddock, however, could not have held on long if Tintin had not succeeded in making radio contact with the battle-cruiser USS *Los Angeles*, which responds, 'Your S.O.S. received. We are coming to your assistance. Will be with you in three hours.'

But the *Ramona* would have been lost if the Curtiss Seahawk SC-1 seaplanes from the Los Angeles – capable of a speed of 290 m.p.h. – had not flown by twenty minutes after the SOS, putting an end to the game of cat and mouse between the submarine and her prey.

In a final attempt to destroy the *Ramona* Kurt sends a frogman armed with a limpet mine, but this plan backfires and the arrival of the *Los Angeles* signals the end of the affair.

During the night, the battle-cruiser then sets course for Jidda to intercept the *Scheherazade*. On the morning of 2 November the yacht is not very far from the Arabian coast as Rastapopoulos manages to make his escape by mini-submarine. During this time the *Ramona* and probably the *Shark* will have been taken over by US Navy detachments and conveyed to Djibouti, where Allan Thompson and his crew, picked up by a Danish cargo, also disembark.

HERGÉ AND MARITIME REGULATIONS

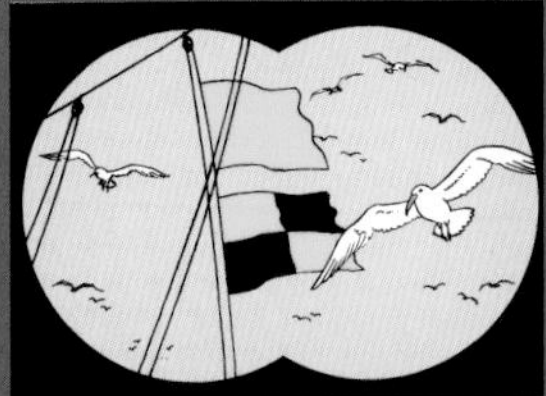

In the current books of* The Adventures of Tintin, *international maritime regulations that demand that every ship should indicate visibly her nationality, her name and her home port are deliberately glossed over.

Like Tintin himself, the ships need to be detached from every geographical context, so that each reader can more easily incorporate them into his or her own imaginary universe.

Early on, Hergé attached less importance to this anonymity. In the first black-and-white edition of *The Broken Ear*, a lifebuoy of the *Ville de Lyon* has the home port clearly inscribed: Le Havre. But in the later colour edition the lifebuoy is blank. In the first edition of *The Black Island* a Belgian flag flies from the prow of the Ostend-Dover ferry. In the second edition the flag is no longer Belgian but black, yellow and black, and in the third edition there is no flag at all.

The exceptions have been carefully considered. The *Ramona* in *The Red Sea Sharks*, for example, is Panama-registered, with all the connotations of a cargo vessel turned 'slaver' flying a flag of convenience.

In his early work, Hergé was not always so careful about observing other maritime regulations, especially concerning navigation lights, but he paid more and more attention to them as he went on.

With *The Prisoners of the Sun* he took extra care over such details. The *Pachacamac* at anchor is very correctly displaying two lights, one fore and one astern, conforming to regulations. As for the 'quarantine' signal, it is given by a combination of flags which, while correct, was not standard.

In *The Red Sea Sharks*, the Ramona sailing at night respects the rules: two mast lights fore and aft, a green lamp on the starboard side, and a red light on the port side. Nevertheless, the mast lights should be at different heights. Moreover, the wheelhouse should never be lit at night.

THE WIRELESS ROOM OF THE SPEEDOL STAR

The wireless room of the *Speedol Star* undergoes a succession of modifications in different editions of *Land of Black Gold*.

In the first version, which appeared in *Le Petit Vingtième* in 1939, a wireless room typical of the end of the inter-war years is depicted. Radio rooms had evolved only very slowly from those to be found on such ships as, for example, the *Titanic*.

In the second (colour) edition that appeared in 1950, the same wireless room is preserved, which seems something of an anachronism. While it is true that some merchantmen which had survived the Second World War would still have been sailing in 1950 using their original equipment, it was no longer the norm. Yet the colouring rejuvenates the drawing.

In the third edition, the wireless room is completely modernized. A comparison of the three drawings shows the attention that Hergé paid to detail. In the first two, the dials and gauges are carefully and accurately copied from pre-war receivers and transmitters; in the third, the radio equipment is functionally stacked in banks and Tintin has the benefit of an extendable lamp.

WESTERMOUTH

THE PORTS

In* The Adventures of Tintin, *one can count some 60 ports across the globe, as well as a dozen imaginary ports invented by Hergé.

Most of the ports are only referred to – such as Reykjavik, the base of the Golden Oil agent in Iceland, or London, to which Chang is bound in *Tintin in Tibet*, or Vigo, in the vicinity of which the steamer *Tanganyika* has sunk in *The Crab with the Golden Claws*.

Some feature only in lists, for instance as stages on the cruise planned by Tintin in the first edition of *Cigars of the Pharaoh*: Port Said, Aden, Bombay, Colombo, Singapore, Hong Kong, and Shanghai. In the subsequent colour edition a different, purely Mediterranean, itinerary is outlined on the map: Tangiers, Algiers, Tunis, Tripoli, Port Said, Piraeus, Istanbul, Naples, Marseilles and Gibraltar.

There are other lists in *The Blue Lotus*. The ships listed on the wall of Mitsuhirato's office are bound for the ports of Marseilles, Antwerp, Le Havre, Rotterdam, Hamburg and Liverpool.

In the first black-and-white edition of *The Blue Lotus* one learns, moreover, that Tintin is returning to Europe aboard the *Rampura* via Hong Kong, Singapore, Colombo, Bombay, Aden, Port Said, Malta, Marseilles, Gibraltar and Southampton.

But an over-fastidious compilation of these references can verge on the absurd, and it is better to concentrate on those ports which either inspired Hergé's drawings or form part of his narrative.

ACTUAL PORTS

Akureyri

A small Icelandic port which is the first stop of the polar vessel *Aurora* in *The Shooting Star*. Shown as it was in the 1940s.

Antwerp

Mentioned only in the early editions. Tintin embarks at Antwerp for the Congo, and the *Aurora* is moored at Wharf 9 there in *The Shooting Star*. The port installations are often recognizable – for example on page 59 of *The Broken Ear*, when Tintin is too late to board the *Washington*, or on page 9 of *The Crab with the Golden Claws*, with the tugboat, tracked quay, cranes and bales (probably of cotton).
Antwerp is the home port of the *Sirius* in *Red Rackham's Treasure*. The ship's cook, Bill, who has already served on board the *Aurora*, lives there. The cranes on rails, the bales of cotton and the docks are depicted on pages 10 and 12.
Antwerp is without doubt the port of departure for the *Speedol Star* in *Land of Black Gold*. From edition to edition the details multiply: tracked quays, rail wagons, cranes, fuel tanks. The main elements of this port scenery are redeployed for other ports across the globe which feature in the adventures.

Callao

The principal commercial and fishing port of Peru, where the *Pachacamac* arrives in *Prisoners of the Sun*. Cranes are shown, and warehouses in the distance. In the foreground are bags of guano for export.
The *Pachacamac* loads the guano for export and brings back from France agricultural machinery in the first edition, and timber in the second.

Chicago

Hergé devotes several pages of *Tintin in America* to the time that Tintin spends in this great lakeside port, capital of Illinois and of the gangster clans. Aside from some views of Lake Michigan, Hergé concentrates on the urban landscape. Apart from the quayside, no port installations are discernible. Moreover, Tintin, who obviously disembarked in New York, arrives in Chicago by train.

Djibouti

Part of two cranes are shown on page 60 of *The Red Sea Sharks* in the newspaper cutting reporting on how the black pilgrims were saved from slavery. We know that it is Djibouti, since this was the port for which Captain Haddock was bound.

Haifa

In the first edition of *Land of Black Gold*, Hergé disguises the name to Caïffa (its ancient name from the time of the crusades), but it later becomes Haifa. The installations of Palestine's main port during the British mandate are scarcely visible, though a Royal Navy launch features.

La Rochelle

This port occupies three pages of the French edition of *The Seven Crystal Balls*. In the English edition it is fictionalized to Bridgeport. Hergé depicts the tracked quayside, a rail wagon, the docks, cargo vessels, warehouses, barrels, sacks and crates, as well as the harbour master's office. However, neither the town nor the actual port is recognizable.

Marseilles

The flying boat coming from the Syldavian coast lands most probably near Marseilles, its destination. Little beyond the aircraft is visible.

New York

Though not mentioned by name, the characteristic Manhattan skyline is instantly recognizable in all editions of *Tintin in America*, as Tintin bids farewell to the New World. For this well-known view, Hergé copied very exactly a newspaper photograph he had kept. It is the only port in all the Tintin adventures which one can recognize at first glance. In the colour edition, Tintin is travelling on the *Normandie*, which sailed the Le Havre-New York route.
In *The Calculus Affair*, New York is also clearly the city represented in the model shown in the presentation and demonstration to the Bordurian chiefs of staff of how a city could be destroyed by ultrasound.

Ostend

Only the quayside and the gangway of the ferry are shown in *The Black Island*. We know that Tintin is at Ostend on account of the early black-and-white edition, where the Ostend-Dover crossing is referred to.

Port Said

This is presented rather vaguely in *Cigars of the Pharaoh*. Cranes and ships can be seen. In the colour edition, the towers of the lighthouse and mosque do not correspond to actual buildings in the Egyptian port.

Saint-Nazaire

This is the port that Hergé drew with the greatest care, using photographs and illustrations that he had collected since well before the war. Altogether, 38 plates in *The Seven Crystal Balls* include elements taken from Saint-Nazaire, which retains its name in the French edition but not in the English version, where it becomes the fictional port of Westermouth. Hergé shows roads, a liner, tugs, the quays, the docks, a pile of coal, the finest cranes to appear in any of the adventures, bales (presumably of cotton), customs officers and sailors.
Hergé's Saint-Nazaire dated from the period when it was a principal port for the liners linking France with Central and South America.

Santa Cruz

The port of Tenerife, this appears in the first black-and-white edition of *Tintin in the Congo*. Tintin gives Snowy a geography lesson: 'You see, Snowy, the Canary Islands are to be found north-west of the Sahara. The port over there is Santa-Cruz.' One can distinguish in the distance the vague silhouettes of a lighthouse and two boats.

Shanghai

The port depicted in *The Blue Lotus* is far from being anonymous like many of the others. Barrels and a sign in Chinese are visible at night, while during the day in the final plate there is a quayside scene full of life, with an attractive junk alongside the liner, cargo vessels, cranes and a warship.
Tintin arrives in and departs from China by Shanghai, its principal port.

THE IMAGINARY PORTS

Hergé had a lot of fun thinking up his imaginary place names, which were often humorous and based on Brussels dialect, but sounding surprisingly realistic. Who would doubt that Dbrnouk in Syldavia is a Balkan port?

Then there is São Rico, a fictitious state whose flag the *Peary* flies in later editions of *The Shooting Star* and perhaps a port too, as the ship is fitted out there. It is also the domicile of the rival expedition's financial backer, the unscrupulous Bohlwinkel.

No matter how convincing it may sound, however, such a port or country does not, of course, exist beyond Hergé's imagination.

Bagghar

Described as 'a large Moroccan port' in *The Crab with the Golden Claws*, this should not be confused with Casablanca. The hinterland is more mountainous, and the Arab quarter is no more reminiscent of Casablanca than of Rabat.

The port facilities are modern, with cranes, quays and warehouses. But the influence of France is omnipresent. Morocco was a French protectorate at the time. The police, the garage mechanics, and the taxi drivers and their customers are all French.

In the first black-and-white edition, the café where Captain Haddock orders drinks has a sign saying 'Café du Port' ('Port Café').

Behind Hergé's invention is the French word 'bagarre', meaning a 'punch-up'.

Bridgeport

The name devised by Hergé's English translators to replace La Rochelle for the English edition of *The Seven Crystal Balls* – reminiscent of the Dorset fishing town of Bridport.

Dbrnouk

This is referred to in the tourist brochure read by Tintin on the aeroplane to Prague in *King Ottokar's Sceptre*. The brochure shows a pipe-smoking fisherman, wearing a red fez and a richly embroidered waistcoat, with a heavy moustache and a gold earring, above the caption 'A typical fisherman from Dbrnouk (south coast of Syldavia)'.

The name sounds very much like that of the Croatian port of Dubrovnik on the Dalmatian coast.

Douma

(Douna in the original black-and-white edition)

This Syldavian port is obscured by the flying boat on which Tintin, Snowy and the Thom(p)sons are embarking. In the original black-and-white edition, more is discernible: the foot of a chain of hills, a lighthouse in the distance, boats and simple port buildings.

Khemikhal

(Khemkhah in the French version)

This punning name was given to the Arab port in the final edition of *Land of Black Gold* – in earlier editions it was either Caïffa or Haifa (see above). Is is the principal port of the imaginary Arab state of Khemed, situated by the Red Sea. The hinterland is more mountainous than that drawn for Haifa – the height of the summits has quadrupled – and there is more port activity. Cranes and cargo vessels are to be seen. The town has been completely Arabized.

As for Khemkhah in the French version, it means 'I'm cold' in Brussels dialect.

Kiltoch

This small Scottish fishing port is elaborated on from edition to edition of *The Black Island*, and from it Tintin sets out to solve the mystery. It ends up with a quay, a jetty, a lighthouse and a few trawlers.

Las Dopicos

Capital of the fictitious republic of San Theodoros, this port is open to the Atlantic and linked to Le Havre by steamship line in *The Broken Ear*. Apart from a liner, sailing vessels, cargo ships, a frigate and a tug can also be identified in its waters. In the final completed adventure, *Tintin and the Picaros*, its name has been changed to Tapiocapolis, after the ruling dictator, but the port area is not shown.

Sanfacion

The capital and port of the South American republic of Nuevo Rico, traditional rival of San Theodoros in *The Broken Ear*. One sees only one street in this port city, and the gangway from the quay to the liner that links the country with Europe.

Wadesdah

Meaning 'What's that?' in Brussels slang, this name has a suitably Arabic flavour for the small seaside town which becomes the capital of Khemed in *The Red Sea Sharks*. Wadesdah is certainly a port, since Allan Thompson wants to disembark Tintin and his two companions there, but it is not as significant as Khemikhal 30 miles away, where the pipeline of this fictitious oil-producing state ends.

The aerodrome of Wadesdah is shown in *The Red Sea Sharks*, and the streets and citadel (also in *Land of Black Gold*), but never the port.

Westermouth

This name – similar to that of the Dorset resort and fishing town of Weymouth – was devised by Hergé's English translators to replace 'Saint-Nazaire' in the original French version of *The Seven Crystal Balls*.

Created by

éditions moulinsart